Fighters Against American Slavery

Other Books in the History Makers Series:

*History*MAKERS

Fighters Against American Slavery

By Stephen R. Lilley

Lucent Books
P.O. Box 289011, San Diego, CA 92198-9011

To Becky, who keeps our world going while I write.

Library of Congress Cataloging-in-Publication Data

Lilley, Stephen R., 1950–
    Fighters against American slavery / by Stephen R. Lilley.
      p.   cm. — (History makers)
    Includes bibliographical references and index.
    Summary: Highlights the careers of leading abolitionists including
Benjamin Lundy, William Lloyd Garrison, Frederick Douglass, Harriet
Tubman, Nat Turner, and John Brown.
    ISBN 1-56006-036-0 (lib. bdg. : alk. paper)
    1. Abolitionists—United States—Biography—Juvenile literature.
2. Antislavery movements—United States—Juvenile literature.
[1. Abolitionists. 2. Antislavery movements.] I. Title. II. Series.
E449.L718   1999
326'.8'092273—dc21
                                                      98-18281
                                                          CIP
                                                           AC

CONTENTS

FOREWORD

The literary form most often referred to as "multiple biography" was perfected in the first century A.D. by Plutarch, a perceptive and talented moralist and historian who hailed from the small town of Chaeronea in central Greece. His most famous work, *Parallel Lives*, consists of a long series of biographies of noteworthy ancient Greek and Roman statesmen and military leaders. Frequently, Plutarch compares a famous Greek to a famous Roman, pointing out similarities in personality and achievements. These expertly constructed and very readable tracts provided later historians and others, including playwrights like Shakespeare, with priceless information about prominent ancient personages and also inspired new generations of writers to tackle the multiple biography genre.

The Lucent History Makers series proudly carries on the venerable tradition handed down from Plutarch. Each volume in the series consists of a set of six to eight biographies of important and influential historical figures who were linked together by a common factor. In *Rulers of Ancient Rome*, for example, all the figures were generals, consuls, or emperors of either the Roman Republic or Empire; while the subjects of *Fighters Against American Slavery*, though they lived in different places and times, all shared the same goal, namely the eradication of human servitude. Mindful that politicians and military leaders are not (and never have been) the only people who shape the course of history, the editors of the series have also included representatives from a wide range of endeavors, including scientists, artists, writers, philosophers, religious leaders, and sports figures.

Each book is intended to give a range of figures—some well known, others less known; some who made a great impact on history, others who made only a small impact. For instance, by making Columbus's initial voyage possible, Spain's Queen Isabella I, featured in *Women Leaders of Nations*, helped to open up the New World to exploration and exploitation by the European powers. Unarguably, therefore, she made a major contribution to a series of events that had momentous consequences for the entire world. By contrast, Catherine II, the eighteenth-century Russian queen, and Golda Meir, the modern Israeli prime minister, did not play roles of global impact; however, their policies and actions significantly influenced the historical development of both their own countries and their regional neighbors. Regardless of their relative importance in the greater historical scheme, all of the figures chronicled in the History Makers series made contributions to posterity; and their public achievements, as well as what is known about their private lives, are presented and evaluated in light of the most recent scholarship.

In addition, each volume in the series is documented and substantiated by a wide array of primary and secondary source quotations. The primary source quotes enliven the text by presenting eyewitness views of the times and culture in which each history maker lived; while the secondary source quotes, taken from the works of respected modern scholars, offer expert elaboration and/ or critical commentary. Each quote is footnoted, demonstrating to the reader exactly where biographers find their information. The footnotes also provide the reader with the means of conducting additional research. Finally, to further guide and illuminate readers, each volume in the series features photographs, a chronology, two bibliographies, and a comprehensive index.

The History Makers series provides both students engaged in research and more casual readers with informative, enlightening, and entertaining overviews of individuals from a variety of circumstances, professions, and backgrounds. No doubt all of them, whether loved or hated, benevolent or cruel, constructive or destructive, will remain endlessly fascinating to each new generation seeking to identify the forces that shaped their world.

A Tiny Minority

The United States is the world's first successful modern democracy. Early in its history, settlers in the thirteen colonies formed governments based on voting and the consent of the people. Even so, when the colonies separated from Britain and issued the Declaration of Independence stating that "all men are created equal," most Americans had accepted slavery for over 150 years. For the next 89 years, America's democratic institutions protected black servitude through custom and law.

From the beginning, only a handful of Americans openly opposed slavery. Americans believed in majority rule, and the majority accepted slavery. The minority that believed in human equality chipped away at this crime against humanity in a long, discouraging battle lasting generations. Some appealed to the con-

Runaway slaves gather for a portrait in Virginia in 1862. The fate of African Americans would be determined by the outcome of the Civil War.

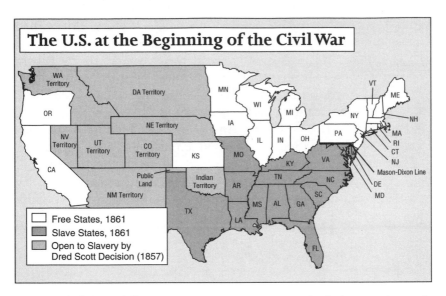

The U.S. at the Beginning of the Civil War

Free States, 1861
Slave States, 1861
Open to Slavery by
Dred Scott Decision (1857)

sciences of their fellow Americans. Some attacked slavery through open rebellion and violence. The stories in this book highlight the careers of five men and one woman who were among this tiny minority. During the last thirty years before the Civil War, public opinion in the northern United States turned increasingly in favor of abolition (the elimination of slavery). In contrast, white southerners defended slavery more energetically during this time. Each of the people described in this book helped mold these opinions and force the conflict that ultimately destroyed black servitude.

These people represent the full range of strategies for ending slavery. The Quaker Benjamin Lundy attempted to convince slave owners that slavery was both a sin and an economic burden. He sought peaceful, gradual emancipation (freedom) for slaves and their resettlement outside the United States. His disciple, William Lloyd Garrison, favored immediate, peaceful emancipation without resettlement.

Born a slave, Frederick Douglass began his fight against slavery by running away from his master. Perhaps more than anyone, Douglass convinced many white Americans that blacks were intellectually suited to be a free people. Harriet Tubman took a more aggressive approach. After running away from slavery, she repeatedly returned to slave territory and smuggled black Americans to freedom. A "conductor" (guide) on the Underground Railroad (a secret system of safe houses and people helping slaves escape), she traveled armed and encouraged slave revolts.

Nat Turner and John Brown represent the violent extreme of antislavery activity. A preacher in rural Virginia, Turner and his fellow slaves formed a conspiracy to massacre whites. Much like Turner, John Brown, a white northerner, intended to arm slaves and lead them in open revolt against their masters. Both Turner and Brown were executed for their troubles. Unlike Lundy, neither hoped to change southern minds, but both helped convince white southerners that there could be no peace between North and South. The fear Turner, Brown, and more peaceful abolitionists inflamed helped start the Civil War, which ultimately ended slavery.

Many other Americans, black and white, male and female, helped to destroy slavery in the United States. Theirs is the story of a dedicated minority who made freedom an ideal cherished by most Americans.

CHAPTER 1

"An Hydra Sin"

Native populations of America and Africa trafficked in slaves among themselves long before whites reached the New World. People of the Iroquois Confederation of eastern North America, the fierce Apache of North America's southwest, and the Aztecs and Mayas of Central America and Mexico all practiced slavery. Pacific northwest tribesmen sometimes displayed their wealth by killing their own slaves.

Europeans Enter the Slave Trade

When Spanish and Portuguese colonists claimed vast New World lands in the fifteenth and sixteenth centuries they lacked sufficient white settlers to develop their hold-ings. They quickly forced natives to labor in their mines and on the es-tates granted by colonial authori-ties. Soon many Spanish settlers found it more profitable to raid the islands and coasts of the Caribbean Sea and Gulf of Mexico for slaves than to prospect for gold.

From the beginning, some Euro-peans opposed enslaving the Indi-ans. Spanish priest Bartolome de Las Casas, the best known critic of Indian enslavement, persuaded Spain's rulers to adopt policies to protect them. In 1517 he suggested Charles I free some Indian slaves by replacing them with black African

During the 1500s Spanish priest Bartolome de Las Casas crusaded against the enslave-ment of Indians.

slaves, a decision the priest later regretted. His recommendation did not cause Europeans to enslave blacks. Spanish merchants had already imported black slaves to the New World.

In the fifteenth and sixteenth centuries, European advantages in wealth, weaponry, and seafaring technology made enslaving Africans relatively easy. More important, native African peoples took part in the trade. Arabs from north Africa captured blacks and sold them into slavery. Black African tribesmen also supplied the coastal trading posts with captives. Some powerful African kingdoms confined white slavers to coastal outposts. Historian Stanley Elkins wrote of one such arrangement:

> Except for the terminal points on the coasts, the trade in slaves was for three centuries rigorously and exclusively controlled by blacks. In Nigeria it was managed by the Oracle, a priestly institution. . . . The prestige of the Oracle, and the class of men that controlled it, enabled this organization to assume control over the trade up and down the entire Niger region. . . . The Oracle . . . condemned hundreds . . . to be sold into slavery, and their disappearance was accounted for locally by the explanation that they had been "eaten" by the Oracle.[1]

Those involved in the trade profited handsomely. Early slave traders at coastal outposts purchased humans for a few trade goods such as knives, scissors, or cloth. One slaver, an Italian-born ship captain who wrote his memoirs under the name Theophilus Conneau, claimed the sale of slaves on his first expedition brought a 100 percent profit for four months' work.

The English Search for Laborers

When profit-hungry English settlers founded Jamestown, Virginia, in 1607 disease, starvation, and Indian attacks thinned the settlers' ranks. The settlement teetered on the edge of disaster. The colony's

Native Africans oversee the transport of captured blacks. Captives would be sold into slavery, becoming the property of wealthy Europeans.

English pilgrims land on the shores of North America. These early settlers relied on indentured servants to fill the ranks of their scanty workforce.

success was assured by the cultivation of tobacco, a crop that made farming so profitable that Virginia settlers planted every cleared patch of land including Jamestown's streets.

In 1618, the Virginia Company began granting fifty acres of land to each person who paid for his own passage to the colony. A settler who brought family members to the colony received an additional fifty acres for each dependent. For many English farmers the chance to own hundreds of acres of rich farmland proved irresistible. Despite the risks of a long sea voyage and life in the wilderness, thousands came.

Soon the English in America faced the same dilemma that the Spanish and Portuguese had—a combination of abundant land and scarce labor. In Virginia, forested land had to be cleared and swampland drained before farming could proceed. Colonial agriculture required intensive labor, but why would a settler work as a hired hand when he could receive a land grant for just coming to Virginia? And by 1618 only seven hundred Englishmen lived in Virginia. Tainted water, hard labor, disease, and warfare with Indians had shortened the average white man's life span to a little over thirty years. Women were scarce in the colony, few children were born, and just over half of the children survived to adulthood. To take advantage of Virginia's rich agricultural possibilities Englishmen resorted to forced labor.

At first, indentured servants supplied the work force. Colonial masters paid the costs of transporting servants to Virginia in ex-

Colonists in Virginia incurred the wrath of outraged Indian tribes when they attempted to enslave Native Americans to compensate for their labor shortage.

change for the workers' pledges to labor for as many as seven years. During the time of service, the master provided for the servant's needs and controlled the servant's life. When the contract period ended, the master would supply clothing and tools to the newly freed servant. In Virginia and other colonies the servant might even obtain free land.

Most servants worked for farmers, and farm work was physically demanding. Some masters also mistreated servants even though colonial laws forbade it. Occasionally, homeless children from English cities were kidnapped and sold into servitude.

Most of Virginia's early settlers came as indentured servants, but the practice had serious drawbacks. Providing for servants' needs was costly. Servants gained freedom at the end of a comparatively short time, and the master then had to find replacements. Young, rebellious servants frequently escaped, blended into society, and started new lives. Indentured servitude proved an imperfect solution to the colonial labor shortage.

English colonists also forced Native Americans into agricultural labor but had little success. Capturing slaves enraged neighboring tribes and brought the risk of war. Indian slaves escaped and returned to their tribes for protection. When colonists sold captured Indians into slavery in the West Indies, often the slaves sickened and died. Tribes of the east coast of North America seldom farmed intensively and left most of the farm work to women. Men accustomed to hunting displayed little aptitude for agricultural tasks. Indian slavery proved impractical for the English colonies.

In 1619, the Jamestown settlers acquired a third source of forced labor when a Dutch warship delivered black African captives to the colony. At first, the colonists considered the blacks indentured servants, but by the 1660s, blacks in the English colonies had become chattel slaves through law and custom. This meant the blacks and their descendants became the property of the masters.

Black slavery brought important advantages to the Virginia planters and other English colonists. Unlike the Indians of eastern North America, blacks from west Africa farmed intensively and men performed the heaviest labor. Africans also possessed knowledge their European masters often lacked. For example, some black Africans knew how to trap and dispose of crocodiles, an important skill in alligator-infested southern colonies.

Just as important, since blacks did not voluntarily emigrate from Africa to America, any black roaming about freely would arouse suspicion. It became unnecessary to mark blacks as slaves because their skin identified them. Even more convenient, black farmers abducted to the English colonies usually lacked the skills to navigate ships to Africa if they escaped. Nor could they expect help from friends, family, or fellow tribesmen if they attempted to escape bondage in the colonies. Help was thousands of miles away.

Slavery Takes Root in the South

English colonists found black slave labor so practical that in the late seventeenth century the Royal

Colonists crowd around to inspect a newly arrived slave during a slave auction in New Amsterdam, New York, in 1643.

African Company was established just to supply the demand. Black slavery spread throughout the thirteen English colonies, but became most deeply rooted in the South. By the early eighteenth century, slave labor had become more common in the heavily agricultural South than indentured servitude. Laborers needed work to keep them busy most of the time, and the plantation system that developed in the South did just that. Large plantations formed self-contained communities where slaves did every kind of work. Slaves served as blacksmiths, carpenters, barrel makers, cobblers, cooks, and seamstresses, but most worked as unskilled field hands cultivating cash crops.

The southern plantation system developed around five cash crops: tobacco, indigo, rice, sugar, and cotton. Since they required

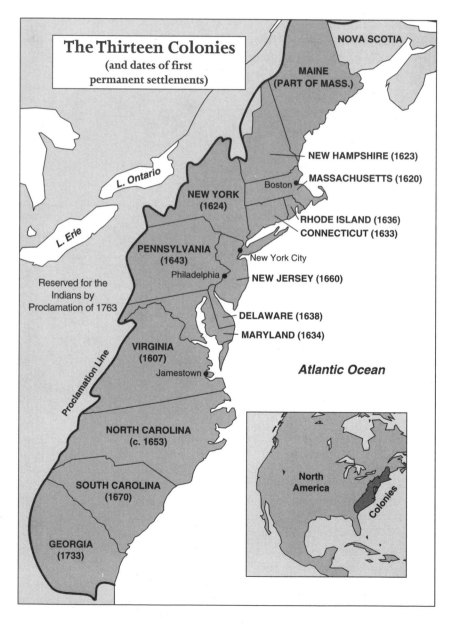

The Thirteen Colonies
(and dates of first permanent settlements)

NOVA SCOTIA

MAINE (PART OF MASS.)

L. Ontario

NEW HAMPSHIRE (1623)

MASSACHUSETTS (1620)

Boston

NEW YORK (1624)

RHODE ISLAND (1636)

CONNECTICUT (1633)

L. Erie

PENNSYLVANIA (1643)

New York City

Philadelphia

NEW JERSEY (1660)

Reserved for the Indians by Proclamation of 1763

DELAWARE (1638)

MARYLAND (1634)

VIRGINIA (1607)

Atlantic Ocean

Jamestown

Proclamation Line

NORTH CAROLINA (c. 1653)

North America

SOUTH CAROLINA (1670)

Colonies

GEORGIA (1733)

huge amounts of inexpensive labor, their cultivation encouraged the use of slaves. While most southern planters were small farmers who owned no slaves, these five crops lent themselves well to production on large plantations. Large-scale production often meant large-scale profits. Historian Clarence Ver Steeg described the process this way:

> Demand for labor rose as southern plantation agriculture expanded. . . . As the supply of slaves was stepped up, the price of slave labor went down. . . . Slavery expanded rapidly with the accelerated pace in the securing of large land grants among the elite in the southern colonies. The first William Byrd [of Virginia] possessed 25,000 acres of land, but his son possessed 175,000 acres. . . . Land. . . was of little or no value until cultivated; to make cultivation possible, labor was needed, and the exploitation of slaves became the accepted answer.[2]

However, even on large plantations each of the five cash crops created its own special set of problems. Wild price swings sometimes made it difficult to profit from tobacco and indigo cultivation. Tobacco also exhausted the soil quickly. Rice and sugar grew successfully only in areas blessed with very long growing seasons. The short staple cotton grown in the southern colonies had seeds that were very difficult to separate from the cotton fibers. The task required so much hand labor that the crop often proved unprofitable. When the cash crops did not provide reliable profits, slavery became an economic burden. After all, masters had to care for their slaves even when they were too young or too old to work profitably. Not only was slavery sometimes unprofitable, it could be dangerous to the master. Those dangers became dramatically apparent in the northern colonies where there were no cotton or indigo fields to keep slaves busy.

Slave Violence

Although major slave uprisings rarely occurred in North America, the possibility terrified the white population. One of the most spectacular revolts erupted in New York City in the spring of 1712. Slaves concocted a magical powder to make them immune to harm and then set fire to part of the city at night. The conspirators killed nine whites and wounded others as the victims stumbled bleary-eyed into the street to fight the fires. Troops suppressed the rebellion, and the convicted conspirators died in grisly public executions.

New Yorkers grew increasingly fearful of slaves following the 1712 uprising, and public executions became common as city officials cracked down on slave conspirators.

For decades afterward, New Yorkers feared such an incident might happen again. When in 1741 it became clear that New York slaves were setting fires, a teenaged white servant girl told city authorities the slaves planned to massacre the white population. With slaves making up one-sixth of the city's population, colonial officials could not ignore the threat. Officials tried accused conspirators and executed twenty-nine blacks and four whites by hanging and burning at the stake. White New Yorkers deported nearly eighty more slaves. If the conspiracy ever really existed, swift action by city authorities crushed the plot.

With some reason, New Yorkers suspected Spanish agents encouraged the 1741 plot. For centuries Britain and Spain had fought occasional wars. On the eve of the 1741 conspiracy, General James Oglethorpe, the founder of Britain's Georgia colony, had warned authorities throughout the English colonies of Spanish agents infiltrating English territory to incite slave revolts. Only two years before, 150 South Carolina slaves murdered some whites and marched toward Spanish Florida. According to Spanish policy, a slave crossing into Spanish territory from foreign soil became free. Even without this refuge, escaped slaves sometimes found sanctuary with Florida's Seminole Indians. Although most slaves peacefully went about their work, many English masters realized trusted servants could turn on them.

Early Opposition to Slavery

Fear of slave violence provided one compelling reason to end slavery in the English colonies, and there were others. Since northern farms produced crops that did not lend themselves well to slave labor, northern masters often had too little work to keep slaves out of mischief. There was even less for slaves to do in northern towns. Also, free northern laborers disliked slave competition. After all, if slaves received only room and board as payment for their work, wages were bound to remain low.

To a number of English colonists it mattered little if slavery were practical, profitable, or legal. To them the issue was simple: slavery was wrong. Many of these early opponents of slavery belonged to a Christian faith called the Society of Friends, more commonly known as "Quakers." Quakers had settled in New Jersey, Rhode Island, and Pennsylvania and firmly believed that the Bible taught nonviolence and human equality. Despite these beliefs, some Quakers owned slaves. In the mid–eighteenth century, Benjamin Lay, John Woolman, and Anthony Benezet called on their Quaker brothers and sisters to oppose slavery.

Lay not only condemned slavery as an insult to God, he used inventive special effects to make his point. Once at a meeting of Friends, Lay waved a sword above his head and shouted that God would be as pleased with their holding humans in bondage as he would with their abusing the Bible. Then for emphasis he ran the sword through the Bible which contained a packet of red dye. The dye, which resembled blood, spattered the shocked onlookers. Now, Lay said, they openly wore the stain of their sins.

John Woolman witnessed one of Lay's outbursts and later read an antislavery pamphlet Lay wrote. After touring North Carolina and witnessing slavery firsthand, Woolman wrote his own essay, "Some Considerations on the Keeping of Negroes." In it he argued that slavery was contrary to God's love and will for Christians. Fellow Quaker Anthony Benezet agreed with Woolman and opened a school for blacks in Philadelphia. Eventually, the Quakers responded to their brothers' opposition to slavery. In 1758, the annual meeting of the Society of Friends in Philadelphia voted to exclude from business meetings any members who bought or sold slaves. After this cautious first step, thirty years passed before the Quakers called on all their members to free their slaves.

American Slavery Versus American Liberty

When the Quakers first voted against slavery, Benjamin Rush was only a boy. Born of Quaker parents on a farm near Philadelphia, Rush became a doctor and gained fame as a member of the Continental Congress and signer of the Declaration of Independence.

In 1773, on the eve of the American Revolution, Rush wrote a vivid essay describing the brutal treatment slaves sometimes suffered. In his essay, he appealed to fellow lovers of liberty to abolish slavery:

> Ye men of sense and virtue, ye advocates for American liberty, rouse up and espouse the cause of humanity and general liberty. . . . Slavery is an hydra sin and it includes in it every violation of the . . . law and the gospel. . . . Remember that national crimes require national punishments. . . . [The crime of slavery] cannot pass with impunity, unless God shall cease to be just or merciful.[3]

Anthony Benezet, the philanthropist who founded a school for blacks in Philadelphia, upheld his Quaker beliefs and condemned slavery.

Years later, Rush wrote that his call for justice caused some of his patients to seek other doctors.

Slavery's evils also troubled the consciences of non-Quakers, including J. Hector St. John de Crevecoeur. A native of France, Crevecoeur admired the American people and settled in New York in 1764. In his widely read book, *Letters from an American Farmer*, Crevecoeur contrasted Americans' love of liberty with the injustice of slavery. Of the southern planters he wrote:

> Their ears by habit are become deaf, their hearts are hardened; they neither see, hear, nor feel for the woes of their poor slaves, from whose painful labours all their wealth proceeds. . . . No one thinks with compassion of those showers of sweat and of tears which from the bodies of Africans, daily drop, and moisten the ground they till. . . .[4]

Other voices cried out for justice for their black brothers and sisters, but they remained a tiny, unpopular minority even though the cause of liberty obsessed the American people. The American Revolution defined freedom for the world but left blacks in slavery. Although blacks fought in the Revolution,

Benjamin Rush urged Americans to oppose slavery out of their love of liberty and sense of moral justice.

two-thirds fought for the British. Britain was more willing to offer slaves freedom than were the patriots.

The Revolution forced many Americans to face the contradiction between slavery and democracy. In fact, few southerners defended slavery as good for either master or slave. George Washington and Thomas Jefferson, both wealthy Virginia slaveholders, condemned slavery. In his will, Washington granted his slaves their freedom. Jefferson would also have done so, but bankruptcy prevented his estate from carrying out his wishes. After the Revolution, Jefferson unsuccessfully urged his fellow Virginians to abolish slavery gradually.

In 1791, southern planter Robert Carter launched an ambitious plan to free his five hundred slaves over a twenty-year period. Hoping the freedmen would earn their own livings, Carter rented small plots of land to them. The project failed. Neighbors complained that the freedmen stole from them or encouraged their slaves to disobey. While Carter freed his slaves partly because of his religious convictions, he undertook his experiment when slaves had become less profitable. Many southern planters criticized slavery more freely as its benefits decreased. Northerners had faced this problem years before.

The United States Government Restricts Slavery

During the Revolution, northern states began abolishing slavery. In 1787, Congress passed the Northwest Ordinance banning slavery in all territories north of the Ohio River and east of the Mississippi. In that same year, the constitutional convention in Philadelphia voted to allow Congress to ban the importation of slaves into the United States as of 1808. Unfortunately, the Constitution also recognized slavery as legal.

In the seventeen years after the constitutional convention, every northern state passed some kind of law freeing slaves, and southern states seemed ready to follow. Southerners found abolition more difficult than northerners because slavery had become part of the South's economic and social system. Freeing all slaves would cost the planters huge sums of money.

Slaves use a cotton gin to process a crop. The invention of the gin caused cotton production to become more efficient and profitable.

Free blacks also frightened white southerners. Would free blacks compete with whites for jobs? Would free blacks become thieves? Would free blacks become savages when whites no longer controlled them? White southerners might have set all these fears aside and freed their slaves had it not been for one invention.

Whitney Makes Slavery Profitable

In 1793, Eli Whitney solved the problem of removing the seeds from short staple cotton. Using his device, the cotton gin, a worker could clean the seeds from cotton fibers in a fraction of the time required to do the task by hand. Cotton production skyrocketed. New England textile mills soon depended on southern cotton. By the mid–nineteenth century, southern states supplied 80 percent of the cotton processed in English mills. On the eve of the Civil War cotton was the United States' most valuable export. The gin also made cotton cultivation the accepted path to wealth, and slavery the accepted system of labor in the South. These events helped create a society in the southern states far different from the northern states. According to historian Charles M. Wiltse:

The factors tending towards southern unity were slaves and cotton. . . . The cotton output had catapulted from three million pounds in 1792, the last year before Whitney's gin had been introduced, to more than thirty-six million pounds in 1800. . . . The South would grow more conservative as her destiny became more deeply involved with cotton and with the . . . system of labor that produced it.[5]

The North and South Debate Slavery

As cotton profits increased, white southerners began to defend slavery and northerners attempted to restrict its spread. When Congress considered admitting Missouri as a slave state in 1819, some northern legislators objected. Although the North had more votes in the House of Representatives, slave and free states had exactly twenty-two votes each in the Senate. Missouri's admission as a slave state threatened the balance. The House passed an amendment proposed by New York Congressman James Tallmadge that would gradually have ended slavery in Missouri, but the Senate rejected it. Instead, Missouri became a slave state and Maine gained admission as a free state. Congress voted to limit slavery in future

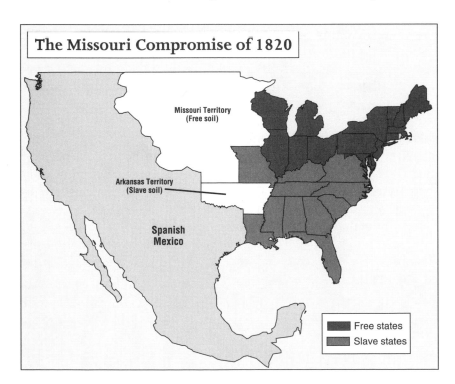

The Missouri Compromise of 1820

Missouri Territory (Free soil)

Arkansas Territory (Slave soil)

Spanish Mexico

Free states
Slave states

states to those territories south of the 36° 30' line. This famous Missouri Compromise settled the dispute momentarily, but it also made something else clear. Americans were choosing sides according to the slavery issue.

A year after Missouri achieved statehood, Reverend Richard Furman wrote South Carolina's governor on behalf of the state's Baptists. Far from arguing as the Quakers had that slavery was un-Christian, Furman argued that the Bible justified slavery. Ten years later, Professor Thomas R. Dew at Virginia's College of William and Mary defended slavery even more strongly. Like Furman, Dew argued that the Bible upheld slavery. Furthermore, he said, blacks were happy as slaves. Dew wrote:

> They are happy and contented, and the master much less cruel than is generally imagined. Why, then, since the slave is happy, and happiness is the great object of all . . . creation, should we endeavor to disturb his contentment by infusing into his mind a vain . . . desire for liberty—a something which he cannot comprehend, and which must dry up the very sources of his happiness.[6]

Dew even argued that slavery helped create a sense of equality among white men since blacks did the least desirable work.

Even after the cotton gin's invention, some white southerners remained unmoved by such arguments. Most of the early–nineteenth-century antislavery societies emerged in upper southern states such as Tennessee, North Carolina, and Virginia. A number of prominent southerners supported the American Colonization Society (ACS). The ACS encouraged masters to free their slaves and raised money to transport freedmen to Africa. There they established a colony called Liberia—the land of freedom.

By the 1830s, even talk of colonization had become unpopular in the South. White southerners defended slavery more uniformly than northerners attacked it. Some critics of slavery wanted to stop slavery from spreading to new territories while others favored immediate emancipation and equality for blacks and whites. Fragmented and disorganized, over the next twenty years slavery's opponents molded themselves into a movement that would change American history.

CHAPTER 2

Benjamin Lundy: Pioneer Abolitionist

When Benjamin Lundy was born in 1789, slavery seemed doomed. Even though United States president-elect George Washington owned hundreds of slaves, his countrymen preached the gospel of freedom. The country had a new constitution that soon would include a strong statement of human rights. Northern states were freeing their slaves, and southerners at least gave the issue serious consideration. These noble impulses soon withered both in North and South when cotton became profitable.

But to Benjamin Lundy, profit mattered less than principle. The child of Quaker parents, he grew to manhood in New Jersey not far from abolitionist John Woolman's home. Like most Quakers, Lundy shared Woolman's antislavery convictions. As a young man he moved south to Wheeling, Virginia, to become a saddle-maker's apprentice. Wheeling lay on a major travel route in the domestic slave trade. Lundy recoiled at the sight of ragged, barefoot people trudging in chains through the mud and snow.

Abolitionist Benjamin Lundy, founder of the Union Humane Society.

Lundy Becomes an Abolitionist

Completing his apprenticeship, Lundy crossed the Ohio River and settled in St. Clairsville, Ohio. Now a married man, his antislavery fervor often distracted him from his family and professional responsibilities. In 1815, he founded an antislavery organization called the Union Humane Society and began corresponding with other fledgling antislavery organizations in the United States.

Lundy's organization took bolder stands than most antislavery societies. The society's beliefs rested on two principles—Jesus' golden rule ("whatsoever ye would that men should do to you, do ye even so unto them,") and the claim of the Declaration of Independence that all men had God-given rights that could not be taken away. The society called on its members to assist and defend free blacks and to promise not to vote for proslavery candidates for public office. Members also pledged to champion black equality, a position rare even for opponents of slavery. Many states had passed laws restricting the rights of free blacks, and the society called for their repeal.

Such reforms would have transformed America, but Lundy and his followers lacked the funds or votes to make them happen. They needed to make converts to their cause. When Tennessee abolitionist Charles Osborn, a fellow Quaker, established his antislavery paper, *The Philanthropist*, Lundy accepted his invitation to help edit the publication. The paper survived only briefly, and the two men soon learned they disagreed on the issue of colonization. From the outset, Osborn rejected colonization as unfair to blacks and harmful to the antislavery cause. Lundy would eventually become the most prominent abolitionist to advocate colonization.

Lundy became a restless, lonely man with a vision. That vision led him to the Missouri territory. Lundy knew Congress had granted Missourians the right to decide whether their state constitution would allow slavery within its borders. He moved his saddle-making business to the territory and campaigned for antislavery delegates. His attempt failed miserably. Proslavery settlers from Virginia and Kentucky had long ago populated the state. The constitutional convention drafted a constitution legalizing slavery, and the Missouri Compromise brought another slave state into the union.

The Genius of Universal Emancipation

His financial resources exhausted, Lundy returned to Ohio and in October 1821, founded an antislavery publication called *The Genius of Universal Emancipation*. The task consumed Lundy completely. He gave up his saddle-making business and traveled from town to town recruiting subscribers for *The Genius*. Issues were printed in Ohio, Tennessee, and in Greenville, North Carolina, a town hosting many antislavery Quakers. Sometimes printers, knowing the unpopularity of the paper's views, refused to work for Lundy. Published whenever Lundy could find a friendly printer that he could afford to pay, *The Genius* continued irregularly until

1839. Often Lundy walked to and from the printers, carrying entire editions in a backpack.

For a time, Lundy published in Tennessee on a press owned by the Tennessee Manumission Society. He chose to operate from a slave state because he hoped to convince southern slaveholders to abandon slavery. Deciding his paper would have more impact if based in a large eastern city, in 1825 Lundy left his family, walked to Baltimore and resumed publication.

In issue after issue, Lundy called for gradual emancipation. Congress, he argued, should use its authority to end the slave trade between states and should abolish slavery in the territories and Washington, D.C. Realizing the Constitution did not permit Congress to interfere in the states' internal affairs, he called for states to send delegates to a convention that would design a national plan for emancipation. Additionally, he proposed eliminating the Constitution's clause recognizing slaves as three-fifths of a person.

In all this, Lundy rejected violence and confrontation. He considered slavery a sin, but did not condemn slave owners as evil. In a spirit of Christian love, he preached antislavery as he would the gospel. Ultimately, he hoped to redeem slave owners by convincing them to free their slaves voluntarily. Wealthy planters reaping huge profits from slave labor had little desire to surrender their workers. On the other hand, while many poor and middle-class white workers hated slavery because it created a class of workers with whom they could not compete, many favored slavery as a way of controlling blacks. Northern laborers also feared an influx of low-wage black workers from the South.

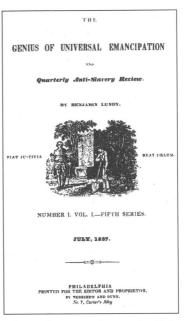

The title page from the July 1837 issue of Benjamin Lundy's antislavery publication The Genius of Universal Emancipation.

The Search for the Promised Land

Realizing racism would probably continue even after emancipation, Lundy favored resettling freed blacks outside the United

Southern slaveholders ignored Lundy's passionate pleas for emancipation, realizing that the abandonment of slavery would cause their profits to plummet.

States. Unlike many who favored colonization, Lundy favored voluntary resettlement because he doubted white citizens would treat black freedmen fairly. If any freed slave preferred to remain in the United States, Lundy argued that the state government should provide education, some land, and full citizenship to the freedmen. Otherwise, slaves should receive financial aid if they chose to emigrate.

Formed in 1817, the American Colonization Society already had begun resettling freedmen, although on a small scale. The ACS attracted some prominent supporters including President James Monroe and later Abraham Lincoln. Many abolitionists denounced the organization as a means of eliminating free blacks from the United States. To these abolitionists, colonization seemed based on the idea that blacks lacked the ability to become capable American citizens. Freed blacks displayed little more enthusiasm for colonization. They viewed Africa as a strange, unknown land and the United States as home.

Despite the obstacles, the society acquired the African territory that would become Liberia and began transporting ex-slaves. Freedmen found farm plots too small to provide them livings. Disease swept away large numbers. Wild animals and hostile native people took their toll. To make matters worse, American blacks enslaved the interior tribes they encountered, a practice that continued into the twentieth century. Historian Clement Eaton declared the entire effort a disaster:

> The American Colonization Society failed miserably in its larger purposes. . . . Despite [its] efforts . . . a relatively small number of Negroes were sent to Africa. . . . The Society transported a total of over 15,000 Negroes between 1821 . . . and 1860. . . . This number was a pitiful fraction of the increase of black babies born in slavery during this period. Thus colonization proved utterly impractical. . . . [7]

But the failure of colonization lay in the future. Despite the strategy's apparent shortcomings, Lundy dedicated himself to establishing a promised land for the freedmen.

The Haitian Experiment

In 1824, Lundy asked the government of Haiti to finance resettlement of ex-slaves. His timing seemed excellent. Haitian president Jean Pierre Boyer wanted colonists to settle his underpopulated republic. Lundy also saw Haiti as proof that blacks could govern themselves. The Haitian government offered full citizenship and civil rights to immigrants, something freedmen could hardly expect in the United States. Just as important, Haiti lay only a few hundred miles from the United States. Settlers could reach the island nation far more economically than they could Liberia. Reports also led Lundy to believe that freedmen would find the Haitian climate more hospitable than Liberia's. Although three of his black friends from Baltimore warned him they opposed colonization, Lundy arranged to transport freedmen to Haiti.

He publicized the plan, insisting that colonization would be necessary only until the United States granted equality to her black citizens. Cleverly, he urged southern planters to free their more rebellious slaves and transport them, a strategy designed to avoid slave revolts. The whole project would cost relatively little. Fifty thousand freedmen could emigrate annually for as little as $720,000, with the Haitian government paying part of the cost.

In September 1824, a number of black leaders in Baltimore met with Lundy and approved the project. North Carolina Quakers transported seven hundred freedmen. The Tennessee Manumission Society pledged its support. Even some planters freed slaves and sent them as colonists. In February 1825, Lundy received word that the initial six thousand colonists were thriving in their new homes.

Unfortunately, the Haitian government soon complained that as many as one-third of the first wave had stayed only briefly and left the colony. Haiti withdrew its financial support. Hoping to continue funding the project, Lundy proposed buying tracts of land in Mississippi and Alabama where slaves could farm and earn money to purchase their freedom. Lundy supported a similar experiment sponsored by feminist Frances Wright in Nashoba, Tennessee.

In addition to funding his Haitian enterprise, Lundy wanted to prove that free blacks worked more efficiently than slaves. On communal farms, free blacks could produce the crops they had grown as slaves. Lundy believed Americans who opposed slavery would surely prefer buying from the freedmen to buying slave goods. Unfortunately, southern planters showed no interest in the scheme. Still determined, in 1826, Lundy left his pregnant, invalid wife and traveled to Haiti to make one last appeal for financial support. The Haitian government refused. Lundy's Haitian adventure failed.

As he prepared to return to Baltimore, he learned that his wife had died giving birth to twins. By now completely obsessed with his antislavery crusade, Lundy left his children with friends and family and became a wanderer. He would not have a home again until the end of his life. According to biographer Merton L. Dillon, the tragedy liberated Lundy, at a terrible cost to his children, to pursue his real ambition:

Exhausted slaves carry in the last crop of the day. Lundy unsuccessfully tried to convince slavers that freed blacks would be more productive workers.

The death of his wife intensified Lundy's attachment to the antislavery cause. His life, long dedicated to the cause of freedom, now became indistinguishable from it. . . . He journeyed thousands of miles within the country and outside it seeking ways to end slavery. But despite such exertions the obstacles to the success of such an undertaking seemed to become greater with every passing year.[8]

Lundy Faces Opposition

As the national debate on slavery intensified, slavery's supporters became less tolerant of abolitionists as meek as Lundy. In 1827, a Maryland slave trader named Austin Woolfolk decided he had had enough of Lundy's antislavery agitation. In January 1827, Woolfolk, already angered by earlier articles in which Lundy had called him a monster, attacked Lundy in the street and nearly beat him to death.

Saved by onlookers, Lundy nursed his wounds for weeks and filed charges against his attacker. When placed on trial, Woolfolk confessed but insisted Lundy's articles had provoked him. After reviewing the articles, the judge agreed, fined Woolfolk one dollar, and encouraged him to file a libel suit against the penniless abolitionist. After the incident, Lundy con-

Lundy persevered in his fight against slavery despite the obstacles he continuously encountered.

cluded that southerners would offer the antislavery cause little support. Increasingly, he turned his attention to the free states.

Now more aware of the physical and legal dangers he faced, Lundy traveled to New England. Depending entirely upon *The Genius* for his income, he recruited new subscribers wherever he went. Often he faced hostility even in the free states. Some Yankee ministers refused to let the little Quaker deliver his lectures in their auditoriums. While in Boston, in 1828, Lundy urged a small group of ministers to take up the antislavery cause. To his surprise, they seemed uninterested. One Unitarian minister told Lundy his constant antislavery agitation might drag the United States into a war between North and South.

Stephen Austin (pictured) issues a land title to colonists in 1822. The Mexican government granted Austin tracts of land in Texas for settlement by Americans.

Although this small, gentle man in dingy clothes made little impression on the group, his speech inspired one young man among them—William Lloyd Garrison. At Lundy's invitation, Garrison edited *The Genius* for a year. While their differing abolitionist philosophies caused them to part, Lundy had planted a powerful seed when he recruited Garrison.

Garrison's opposition to colonization caused the rift with Lundy. Lundy never abandoned the idea and searched tirelessly for a place to settle the freedmen. In 1830, he claimed his journeys had covered twenty-five thousand miles. Over the years, he visited nineteen states, paying his own expenses or depending on the charity of friends and colleagues. Seeking a safe haven for the freedmen, he traveled to Haiti a second time in 1829, and three times to Mexican Texas between 1830 and 1835.

In 1832 he traveled to Canada in disguise for his own safety. While there, Lundy visited a black settlement established by English abolitionist and philanthropist William Wilberforce. Wilberforce's colony disappointed Lundy. In that harsh northern climate, Lundy found the impoverished black settlement torn by internal disputes.

Hope for a Texas Colony

For a time, Texas offered the best prospect for black settlement. During his stay in Missouri, Lundy had lived in Herculaneum, home of Moses and Stephen Austin. There he learned that the Mexican government had granted the Austins sizeable tracts of land for settlement in Texas. When in 1829 the new Mexican republic had abolished slavery, Lundy saw Texas as a potential home for freedmen. Bordering the United States, Texas could easily be reached and it possessed vast expanses of rich farmland. More important, few whites lived there, reducing the chances freedmen would suffer persecution.

From 1832 to 1835, Lundy sought Mexican approval for a black settlement. The journey across the frontier wilderness took a terrible toll on the frail abolitionist's health and exhausted his financial resources. Although he sometimes traveled in disguise, Texas slaveholders occasionally learned his identity and threatened his life. After years of negotiations, the Mexican government agreed to grant land to black settlers and a generous tract for Lundy's personal use. Overjoyed, Lundy planned for the black exodus but fell seriously ill shortly after he returned to the United States. A brief stay in jail for nonpayment of debts further delayed the freedmen's exodus. The trip to the promised land would have to wait.

Unfortunately, hundreds of slave-owning families from the United States had already settled in Texas. When Mexican dictator Antonio Lopez de Santa Anna attempted to tighten his control over the territory, the Texans revolted and won their independence in 1836. The Mexican government could no longer keep its promise to Lundy. The dream of a free black settlement in Texas died.

Mexican troops battle Texas colonists at the Alamo. Lundy's hope for a free black colony in Texas was crushed when colonists won their independence in 1836.

The Fight to Block Texas Statehood

Independence for Texas meant the birth of a new slaveholding nation. In *The Genius* Lundy correctly predicted that Texas would soon become a slave state. Former president John Quincy Adams, now a congressman from Massachusetts and determined opponent of slavery, admired Lundy's articles. During debates in the House of Representatives over whether to annex Texas, Adams quoted Lundy's writings at length. Later, Adams met Lundy and discussed the annexation issue with him.

Encouraged by Adams's attention, Lundy founded a new antislavery magazine, *The National Enquirer*, in Philadelphia. He also helped found the Pennsylvania Antislavery Society. Despite Adams's and Lundy's efforts, Congress voted to annex Texas in 1845. While Lundy lost the battle to block the annexation, the effort marked the zenith of his career. His health failing and his money gone, he left the editorial duties at *The National Enquirer* to abolitionist author John Greenleaf Whittier and planned to join his children in Illinois.

Storing his personal belongings in Pennsylvania Hall, Lundy prepared for his journey. Before he left, an antislavery group composed of blacks and whites, men and women met in the hall. A mob, angered by the mingling of races and sexes, burned the building. The flames consumed Lundy's possessions including most of his personal papers. Stripped of everything, Lundy regained custody of his children and settled on a small farm. As the national debate over slavery approached its climax, he lived quietly there until his death in 1839.

Former president John Quincy Adams (pictured) supported Lundy's opposition to slavery and fought to prevent the Union from annexing Texas.

Dreams Unfulfilled

Lundy's dream of a peaceful end to slavery might have come true if all abolitionists had addressed the issue with the same love and moderation he did. On the other hand, by the end of Lundy's career, slave owners tolerated no criticism. In fact, Lundy's moderate plan of gradual emancipation and colonization angered both sides in the debate. According to historian Dwight Lowell Dumond:

By 1829 gradual emancipation was recognized as imperfect, inequitable, and indecisive, and colonization was known to be a complete failure. . . . Men like James G. Birney [and] Gerrit Smith . . . publicly rejected colonization. . . . Southerners moved with equal resolution to defend slavery and to silence all antislavery arguments even though coupled with colonization. Lundy was trapped by his inability to face reality.[9]

Lundy ended his life revered as a pioneer in antislavery circles. Abolitionists recognized his sincerity and dedication but rejected his methods. Historian Henrietta Buckmaster believed Lundy's greatness overshadowed his failures:

His accomplishments were small, his scope was limited, but he represented with a homely grandeur the love of justice which makes a great man. He knew that every voice raised in protest, every effort to draw together a shield of friends, forged a strong and sturdy cooperation between the races.[10]

Decades after Lundy's death, the races cooperated to destroy slavery in a bloody civil war. That war came in part because one of his disciples deepened the distrust between North and South. Lundy had preached love. His disciple preached judgment.

CHAPTER 3

William Lloyd Garrison: The Uncompromising Abolitionist

Few people see their world with absolute certainty. William Lloyd Garrison was such a man. Born in Massachusetts in 1805, Garrison had two things in common with the Puritans who stepped ashore at Plymouth in 1620—an inflexible sense of mission and a determination to do what he considered right.

Much of this he inherited from his mother, a deeply religious woman. Once an Episcopalian, she became a zealous Baptist, causing her parents to reject her. Her hard-drinking husband abandoned the family early in William's childhood. Molded by his mother's influence, William considered the Bible God's perfect word and strove for spiritual perfection. For a time, he considered becoming a missionary.

At first, he seemed destined for humbler work. His mother unsuccessfully apprenticed him to two cobblers. A later apprenticeship with a cabinet maker ended when young William ran away. The experiences gave the boy a mild taste of servitude. His apprenticeship under a printer proved more successful. William enjoyed the work and educated himself while setting type. He

Even as a young man William Lloyd Garrison displayed the qualities that would later make him an illustrious abolitionist: determination and moral righteousness.

learned so well that he wrote anonymous articles, some of which his employer published. Lacking formal education or wealth, William had acquired a means to mold his world—the printed word.

Garrison Enters the Abolitionist World

Garrison's skill as a printer and writer brought him to Boston where he became editor of the *National Philanthropist*, the first publication in the United States dedicated to ending the use of alcoholic beverages. While the paper survived only one year, it brought him to the attention of abolitionist Benjamin Lundy. Lundy's appeals for the freedom of all men and women inspired the crusading Garrison. Garrison embraced abolitionism although he knew little of slavery. At Lundy's invitation he became the editor of *The Genius of Universal Emancipation* in 1829.

At first, Garrison accepted Lundy's idea that emancipation must come gradually and that free blacks would have to settle outside the United States. After reading British antislavery pamphlets, Garrison's philosophy began to change. Captivated, he followed news reports of debates in Britain's Parliament about immediate emancipation in the West Indian colonies. By comparison, Lundy's gradualism and moral appeals seemed puny.

Garrison concluded that gradual emancipation and colonization wronged slaves. If God considered all people equal, he argued, blacks deserved immediate freedom and full United States citizenship. Garrison decided that if Americans truly loved liberty they must educate blacks and give them religious training to prepare them for citizenship. These views found their way into Garrison's articles and drove subscribers away from *The Genius* at an alarming rate. Lundy had based his paper in Maryland partly because he wanted to carry the abolitionist argument directly to the slave states, but Baltimore's slave traders did not take sharp criticism of the slave trade lightly. Garrison soon discovered this.

Discarding Lundy's gentle appeals to the consciences of proslavery whites, Garrison published uncompromising antislavery editorials including an article condemning as a murderer and a thief a ship owner whose vessel transported slaves. A Baltimore court found Garrison had libeled the ship owner and fined him fifty dollars. Unable to pay, Garrison remained in jail until a wealthy New York abolitionist, Arthur Tappan, paid the fine.

The Liberator

Realizing they no longer shared the same philosophy of abolitionism, Garrison and Lundy agreed to go their separate ways. In January 1831, Garrison launched his own antislavery publication, *The Liberator*, in Boston. The enterprise hardly looked promising. Initially, he had no subscribers. Always short of money, Garrison

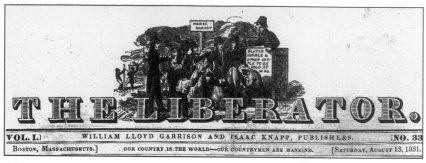

The title The Liberator *stands boldly on the front page of the August 13, 1831, edition of Garrison's antislavery newspaper.*

printed the paper on borrowed equipment and slept on the floor next to the press. Despite this, his first issue harshly scolded the North for its prejudice and apathy concerning slavery. Boldly, Garrison demanded immediate freedom for all slaves:

> On this subject I do not wish to think, or speak, or write with moderation. No! No! Tell a man whose house is on fire to give a moderate alarm; tell him to moderately rescue his wife from the hands of the ravisher [rapist]; tell the mother to gradually extricate her babe from the fire into which it has fallen—but urge me not to use moderation in a cause like the present. I am in earnest; I will not equivocate; I will not excuse; I will not retreat a single inch— AND I WILL BE HEARD.[11]

These would be the most famous words Garrison would ever write. *The Liberator* would make him the leading voice of the American abolition movement.

This sort of notoriety brought risks. In August 1831, a Virginia slave named Nat Turner led the worst servile insurrection in decades. Turner and his followers murdered dozens of whites. Anxious to influence southerners, Garrison had sent free copies of *The Liberator* to people in the South. Open slave revolts rarely occurred in the United States. Many southerners blamed *The Liberator's* harshly worded call for immediate emancipation for the revolt. Although personally opposed to violence of any sort, Garrison denied he encouraged the revolt but defended it as equivalent to the acts of American patriots in the American Revolution. In the month following Turner's revolt, Garrison wrote in *The Liberator*:

> Ye accuse the pacific [peaceful] friends of instigating the slaves to revolt. . . . The slaves need no incentive at our

hands. They will find them in their stripes—in their ema-
ciated bodies—in their ceaseless toil . . . in every field, in
every valley . . . wherever you and your fathers have
fought for liberty—in your speeches, your conversations,
your celebrations . . . invitations to resistance above,
below, around them! What more do they need? . . . They
deserve no more censure than . . . our fathers in slaughter-
ing the British.[12]

Inciting slave revolt was a criminal offense in the South. South
Carolina governor Robert Hayne asked Boston's mayor Harrison
Gray Otis to close the paper. Georgia offered a $5,000 reward for
Garrison's arrest. Neither attempt to silence Garrison succeeded,
and the abolitionist's actions over the next thirty years did noth-
ing to improve white southerners' opinions of him.

A Lack of Support

Had Garrison continued to call for colonization of freed slaves
in Africa, his message might have appealed to a wider audience.
Many white southerners opposed slavery but did not want to
live with free blacks. Garrison
now condemned colonization as
anti-Negro. Any freed blacks who
agreed to settle in Africa he
branded traitors to their race. Garrison's extreme rhetoric isolated
him from many abolitionists. This
isolation became obvious when
Garrison formed the New England
Anti-Slavery Society in December
1831. Only ten people attended
the organizational meeting.

This lack of support only seemed
to reassure Garrison of his own
righteousness. Undaunted, he traveled to England in May 1833, using
funds obtained from the New England Anti-Slavery Society. Suppos-
edly, he intended to collect

*An 1835 engraving of Garrison
depicts the abolitionist at age
thirty. Around this time, Garrison fervently worked to raise
funds for and awareness of the
antislavery cause.*

contributions from wealthy English abolitionists for black education in the United States and to encourage the English to oppose
the American Colonization Society. In fact, other American abolitionists had already contacted the English for both these purposes.

Garrison not only failed to raise the funds but had to borrow money for the return trip to the United States. Garrison's trip accomplished little more than promoting William Lloyd Garrison.

He may have intended this from the beginning. After this trip, many English abolitionists considered him America's leading abolitionist. Since American abolitionists looked to the better-established English antislavery movement for guidance, Garrison's acceptance by the British movement bolstered his stature at home. While Garrison acquired valuable connections with English abolitionists, trusting blacks had helped finance the trip expecting very different results. His patrons' hard-earned money may have produced little more than America's most hated abolitionist.

Garrison and the Antislavery Societies

At least Garrison had become a powerful irritant, constantly harassing proslavery forces and sometimes inspiring abolitionists. While Garrison neither lobbied for emancipation legislation nor smuggled slaves to freedom, the loudest appeals for abolition came from his voice and his pen. In December 1833, he used his magnified prestige to help organize the American Anti-Slavery Society. If he hoped to dominate the organization, he was disappointed. Fearful of his radical influence, more moderate delegates to the organizational meeting assigned Garrison the task of communicating with international antislavery societies. He also drafted the organization's statement of principles. The statement called for immediate emancipation worldwide without payment to slave owners, for legal recognition of full black equality, for the creation of local antislavery societies, and for an ambitious program of antislavery propaganda.

The title page of an 1840 almanac published by the American Anti-Slavery Society.

More than anything, Garrison contributed speeches, articles, and propaganda to the antislavery cause. In October 1835, the Boston Female Anti-Slavery Society invited Garrison and an English abolitionist, George Thompson, to address one of their

THOMPSON,
THE ABOLITIONIST.

That infamous foreign scoundrel **THOMPSON**, will hold forth *this afternoon*, at the **Liberator Office, No. 48, Washington Street.** The present is a fair opportunity for the friends of the Union to *snake Thompson out!* It will be a contest between the Abolitionists and the friends of the Union. A purse of **$100** has been raised by a number of patriotic citizens to reward the individual who shall first lay violent hands on Thompson, so that he may be brought to the tar kettle before dark. Friends of the Union, be vigilant!

Boston, Wednesday, 12 o'clock. Oct 21. 1835

A flyer posted by anti-abolitionists calls for "friends of the Union" to capture and tar abolitionist George Thompson.

meetings. Partly due to its long involvement in the cotton trade, Boston harbored some violent slavery supporters. Yankees especially resented Englishman Thompson and his criticisms of their institutions. Warned that a mob might handle him roughly if he delivered his speech, Thompson quietly left town before the meeting.

Garrison arrived as scheduled and blundered into an angry group of men threatening the women hosting the meeting. After momentarily quieting the men, at the ladies' request he slipped away to the Anti-Slavery Society's office in that building. The calm lasted only briefly. The little handful of women held their ground in the face of a mob numbering in the thousands, but the unruly protesters forced the meeting to adjourn. Still hungry for prey, the mob crashed into Garrison's office just as he leaped out a window. Friends concealed him behind a pile of lumber, but the mob soon discovered him and dragged him into the street. The protesters dragged Garrison along, some tearing the clothes from his body, some screaming that he should be lynched.

Two strong men took him in hand insisting that no one should harm a fellow American. Marching at the head of the crowd, they delivered Garrison to Boston's mayor who thrust him into a horse-drawn cab and jailed him for safekeeping. Later, Garrison noted ironically that in the birthplace of the American Revolution a mob had attacked people committed to the cause of freedom.

41

An angry mob of slavery supporters drags Garrison through the streets of Boston. The incident brought increased attention to the slavery debate.

I was . . . conducted over the ground that was stained with the blood of the first martyrs in the cause of LIBERTY and INDEPENDENCE, by the memorable massacre of 1770 [the Boston Massacre]. . . . What a scandalous and revolting contrast! My offence was in pleading for . . . liberty for my enslaved countrymen, colored though they be—liberty of speech and of the press for ALL. And upon that "consecrated spot" I was made an object of derision and scorn.[13]

The incident dramatized Garrison's role in the abolitionist world. His constant goading of slavery's supporters brought out the worst in them. Every southern demand for his arrest, every mob action against him, every attempt to keep *The Liberator* from circulating in the South reminded many Americans that they could not maintain both slavery and their own cherished freedoms.

Garrison flourished in his role as antislavery's lightning rod, becoming even less tolerant of disagreement. He condemned national church organizations for not ending their association with slave-holding congregations in the South. Garrison called church leaders who tolerated their slave-holding brethren thieves, pirates, and adulterers, language that offended even abolitionists. Garrison had taken Jesus' command to be perfect seriously. Whether Garrison's beliefs grew from biblical teaching, his own huge ego, or a mixture of the two, he proclaimed them loudly.

Not only did he seek purity in his antislavery beliefs, he embraced other controversial causes. He preached pacifism (nonviolence) claiming that even self-defense was unjustified. When in 1837 abolitionist Elijah Lovejoy died in a gun battle against a proslavery mob in Alton, Illinois, Garrison criticized Lovejoy for taking up arms. He also called for the prohibition of alcoholic beverages, and for social and legal equality for women.

Many of the American Anti-Slavery Society's most influential members supported women's equality but thought the organization should focus its attention strictly on antislavery. Much to his opponents' dismay, Garrison packed the society's 1840 convention with his supporters. The delegates promptly chose Garrison as the society's president, assuring conflict within the membership. Unhappy with Garrison's radicalism, many members, including James Birney and Theodore Weld, left the society. Later they formed a rival organization, the American and Foreign Anti-Slavery Society.

No Union with Slaveholders

Despite his victory at the 1840 convention, Garrison ruled only the ruins of the American Anti-Slavery Society. With his opponents' departure, the organization lacked real national influence but became increasingly radical. In May 1844, the American Anti-Slavery Society resolved that the free states should form a separate union from the slave holding states. Remaining in a union with slave states, Garrison argued, tainted the northern states with southern sins.

Garrison believed bloody slave revolts would eventually sweep across the South. If free states seceded from the slave states, northern troops could not be called to suppress southern slave insurrections. Secession would also leave slaveholders no legal way to recover runaways who sought refuge in the North.

This doctrine attacked a document most Americans revered almost as much as the Bible—the United States Constitution. Garrison denounced the Constitution because it allowed southern states to count three-fifths of their slaves for representation in Congress. This amounted to official recognition of slavery. Since no slave could vote or hold office, the three-fifths clause mainly benefited slaveholders and did nothing for the slaves.

Three millions of the American people are crushed under the American Union! They are held as slaves—trafficked as merchandize—registered as goods and chattels! The government gives them no protection—the government is their enemy—the government keeps them in chains. . . . The Constitution which subjects them to hopeless bondage, is one that we cannot swear to support! Our motto is, "NO UNION WITH slaveholders." [14]

Garrison incorporated the slogan into his speeches, often publicly burning a copy of the Constitution for emphasis.

Garrison's rejection of the Constitution may have moved him closer to the spiritual purity he craved, but it moved him farther from a real solution to the problem. The type of political activism used by abolitionists such as James Birney, Theodore Weld, and Frederick Douglass helped bring about such sweeping changes as the creation of the Republican Party, Abraham Lincoln's election to the presidency, and the end of slavery. In contrast, Garrison and his followers refused either to vote or hold political office. They stood aloof from the crime of slavery, morally pure but politically insignificant.

Like an Old Testament prophet, Garrison's fiery speeches called down God's judgment on the United States for not freeing all her people. He condemned the annexation of Texas in 1845 because it expanded slavery westward. He condemned the Compromise of 1850 because its tougher Fugitive Slave Law endangered the freedom of all blacks living in the North. He condemned the Kansas-Nebraska Act in 1854 because it allowed citizens of a territory to legalize slavery in a new state. He supported John Brown's Harper's Ferry raid in 1859 despite his pacifist principles. Although he stung the nation's conscience, he fought a war of words while others toiled and risked their lives to free an oppressed people.

The Civil War

Abraham Lincoln's election to the presidency in 1860 triggered the real war to end slavery. With Lincoln's election, southerners feared slavery's days were numbered. Seven southern states seceded and formed the Confederate States of America. On April 15, 1861, Confederate artillery bombarded United States troops at Fort Sumter in Charleston, South Carolina. The Civil War had begun. Pacifist or not, Garrison supported the war. He had hoped slaveholders would answer his call to righteousness, repent, and free their slaves. Now slaveholders' violence against black people brought violence down on the South. Four days after the war began, Garrison wrote:

> Now that civil war has begun . . . it is for the abolitionists to "stand still and see the salvation of God," rather than attempt to add any thing to the general commotion. It is no time for . . . criticism of Lincoln, Republicanism, or even the other parties, now that they are fusing for a death grapple with the Southern slave oligarchy; for they are instruments in the hands of God to . . . achieve the great object of emancipation, for which we have so long been striving.[15]

Disturbed by Lincoln's continued insistence that the United States would fight the war not to free slaves but to restore the Union, Garrison campaigned for a war to end slavery. When in January 1863, Lincoln's Emancipation Proclamation declared all slaves in rebel-held territory free, Garrison realized slavery could not survive anywhere in the United States.

A Prophet of Liberty

The war and emancipation changed Garrison's public image from that of an angry radical to that of a prophet of liberty. After the Confederates surrendered, Garrison was asked to attend the ceremony at which the United States flag was raised over Fort Sumter. Only a few years earlier, Garrison would have faced arrest or death had he traveled to the South. Now, freedmen at the ceremony surrounded the old abolitionist, raised him above their heads, and paraded him triumphantly through the streets of Charleston.

The 1860 election of President Abraham Lincoln foreshadowed the end of slavery in the United States.

With the ratification of the thirteenth amendment to the Constitution, slavery ended. Garrison stopped publication of

The Liberator and proposed disbanding the American Anti-Slavery Society, a proposal its membership rejected. Garrison thought the society had outlived its usefulness. In a letter to his wife he implied that some abolitionists only wanted to preserve the society for their own benefit:

> I regard the whole thing as ridiculous; and I am quite sure that this determination to go on is not the result of any conviction but . . . arises from . . . an ulterior purpose. . . . I shall rejoice when it is all over.[16]

For the remainder of his life, he turned his attention to other matters including eliminating trade barriers between nations. Garrison died in New York in May 1879, hailed as a great American.

Garrison's Contributions

Garrison's contribution to the antislavery struggle is difficult to measure. He did not aid runaways, sponsor legislation to end slavery, or seek public office. His bitter attacks on slave owners may have made them more determined to keep their slaves. According to historian Dwight Lowell Dumond:

> Garrison's intemperate language regarding the Constitution and government of the United States, and his ultimate refusal to vote . . . hurt the cause of emancipation. . . . It played into the hands of pro-slavery men. It was an obstacle to political action against slavery. It split the American Anti-Slavery Society. . . . He made a contribution. It was neither a large or an overpowering one, and sometimes it was a negative one.[17]

Garrison's uncompromising manner never swerved from its ultimate goal: the abolition of slavery in the United States.

Garrison's refusal to compromise on the slavery issue both helped and hurt the abolitionist cause. Slave owners might have found calls for gradual emancipation less offensive. But southern leaders understood both immediate and gradual abolition threatened to destroy their way of life. Tact would have accomplished little. Garrison's harsh words became salt rubbed into the open wound that was slavery. Garrison forced America to face the great moral crime of slavery honestly. Criticized as arrogant and self-righteous, he could no more have compromised with slavery than he could have with the devil.

On the other hand, Garrison inspired and recruited antislavery giants such as Wendell Phillips and Frederick Douglass. Douglass, a runaway slave, considered Garrison "the foremost, strongest, and mightiest among those who have completely identified themselves with the Negroes in the United States."[18] He could have been speaking of himself.

Frederick Douglass: The Voice of His People

The leading black abolitionist of the 1800s began his career by freeing one slave—himself. Frederick Douglass was a runaway slave. According to some estimates, by the mid-1800s twenty-seven thousand slaves fled annually, leaving homes and families behind. More remarkably, the vast majority of slaves, millions of able-bodied, intelligent people, did not escape during almost three centuries of slavery. Most who did attempt escape succeeded. After all, slaves were rarely locked up or chained. But slavery forged invisible chains.

Most slaves could not read or write. For them, reading maps and road signs or making false travel passes and freedom papers was out of the question. Illiterate people also knew less about the ideas of equality expressed in the Declaration of Independence and the Bible. These documents, which inspired rebellion and resistance in others,

Frederick Douglass embarked on a crusade to free blacks from the bonds of slavery.

were less accessible to slaves. Every day's experience reminded the black slaves they were meant to be a white man's property. Every day slaves learned that their white masters wielded power they could never match. The slaves' ignorance magnified the white man's power. Escaping slaves blundered through a hostile world by night, uncertain of their paths, guided only by the North Star, and trusting strangers to help them. Escape became even more difficult if a slave tried to bring family along. Frederick Douglass would find it easier to escape. He would have no family to complicate his escape and his home would lie on the edge of freedom.

Douglass Faces the Reality of Slavery

Born in 1817 in Talbot County, Maryland, near Chesapeake Bay, Frederick began life with an extravagant name—Frederick Augustus Washington Bailey. He knew little of his mother, seeing her only four or five times in his life. As for his father, Frederick knew only that he was a white man. His grandparents, Isaac, a free black man, and Betsy ("Grandma Betty") Bailey, a slave woman, raised Frederick until he reached seven years old.

One day, without explaining where they were going, Grandma Betty took Frederick for a long walk. The seven-year-old soon found himself in unfamiliar territory. Frederick recalled fear rising in his heart with each step he took from home. Every log and limb became a monster by the roadside. Sometimes, Grandma Betty carried the nervous little boy. At last, they reached Captain Aaron Anthony's plantation, one of many he owned. There Frederick saw a large yard filled with children, most black, some light skinned but not white. When several of the children invited him to play he refused. Grandma Betty pointed out Frederick's brother and sisters, none of whom he had ever met, and encouraged him to join the children. Reluctantly, Frederick followed the children behind a house and watched them at play. Soon, one ran up to him and shouted "Fed, Fed, grandmama gone!"

Suddenly he found himself separated from the only family he had ever known. "Old Master," as the slaves called Captain Anthony, found it more efficient to place all slave children in one location when they reached the age of seven or eight. This freed adults from parental distractions and enabled one slave to attend to many children.

On Old Master's plantation, a slave woman called Aunt Katy supervised many of the children. She instantly disliked Frederick and as punishment often starved him. The boy recalled fighting off hunger by snatching table scraps. At the end of one of those long days without food, Frederick sat crying by the fireplace as he watched Aunt Katy feed slices of bread to the other children. He had concealed a few kernels of dry corn he intended to eat when his tormentor was not watching.

As if by magic, his mother appeared in the kitchen and knelt by her sobbing son. She had walked twelve miles after a full day's work to visit Frederick. The boy explained why he was crying. His mother, a tall, strong, handsome woman, rose, faced Aunt Katy,

49

As a slave on a southern plantation, Douglass witnessed firsthand the cruelties of slavery. Here, young Frederick watches as a fellow slave is brutally whipped.

and warned her in menacing tones that she expected her son to receive better treatment. Leaving Katy, she gave Frederick a ginger cake and cradled him in her lap as he ate. Frederick fell asleep in his mother's arms. When he awoke she was gone. He never saw her again. Soon after this visit, he learned his mother had died. If separation from his family caused Frederick deep emotional pain, it also helped break his attachment to life as a slave. One of the invisible chains was loosened.

Frederick learned much about slavery at his new home. Once he saw a young woman stumble onto Old Master's plantation, her body torn and bleeding. Although she had been beaten by a drunken overseer, the master angrily ordered her back to work.

Douglass saw another woman whipped with forty lashes, each stroke cutting deep into her flesh. Frederick also experienced kindness on occasions. His master's daughter sometimes fed him slices of bread when he sang for her. Once when Frederick suffered injuries in a fight, she bandaged his head.

A New World

The attachment to his mistress did not last long. Often Maryland planters had more slaves than they could profitably employ, so in 1825, Frederick's master sent him to Baltimore. There he worked as a house servant for one of his master's relatives, Hugh Auld. Baltimore opened a new world to him. When Frederick heard his mistress, Sophia Auld, reading the Bible he asked her to teach him to read. She agreed and took pride in his rapid progress. When her husband learned of the lessons he scolded his wife in little Frederick's presence. Book learning, he explained, would ruin even the best slave.

When the lessons ended, Sophia Auld did her best to keep the boy from obtaining reading material, an impossible task. He collected discarded scraps of books wherever he could find them. With the pennies he earned from shining boots he bought a schoolbook filled with speeches about the rights of man, which he read and memorized. Frederick also secretly bribed schoolboys with food in exchange for lessons in reading and writing. Lacking paper, he practiced writing on fence boards with bits of charcoal. Sophia Auld had stirred Frederick's hunger for knowledge. She had loosened another of the invisible chains, for without increased knowledge Frederick might have accepted his servitude.

Mrs. Auld teaches Frederick how to read. Her husband, Frederick's master, quickly put an end to the lessons, fearing education would ruin his slave.

Hugh Auld put Frederick to work as an unskilled ship builder, a job more agreeable and interesting than field work on the plantation. Frederick ate well and wore better clothes than he had on the plantation. His master never whipped him and allowed him to

51

travel freely throughout the city. But Frederick also saw those less fortunate. He saw slaves loaded like cattle onto ships bound for the deep South. Increasingly, Frederick considered escaping. More important, he began to think of fighting slavery's injustices. Then in 1833, he read a newspaper article about petitions filed in Congress against slavery. The idea that other people opposed servitude thrilled him. But for the moment, Frederick benefited little from the national debate about slavery.

Covey the Slave Breaker

In the upper South, especially Maryland and Virginia, masters constantly bought and sold slaves or tried to find them employment that would make them profitable. Frederick soon found himself back on the plantation under the control of Old Master's son-in-law, Thomas Auld. During his stay in Baltimore, Frederick had moved about freely and had performed mostly light work. More important, his secret reading had filled his head with ideas of freedom. Auld found his young slave so spoiled by the freedom he had enjoyed in Baltimore that he hired Frederick to a professional slave breaker, Edward Covey. Covey attempted to crush Frederick's spirit by overwork and starvation. In his autobiography, he admitted Covey had destroyed his spirit:

> I was somewhat unmanageable at first, but a few months of . . . discipline tamed me. Mr. Covey succeeded in *breaking* me—in body, soul, and spirit. My natural elasticity was crushed; my intellect languished; the disposition to read departed, the cheerful spark that lingered about my eye died out; the dark night of slavery closed in upon me.[19]

Finally nearing the limits of his endurance, Frederick ran away from Covey for two days. When he returned, Covey attempted to whip the rebellious sixteen-year-old, but Frederick wrestled the slave breaker to the ground. The resistance astonished Covey. When Covey's cousin attempted to interfere, Frederick kicked him so savagely he retreated. After this, no one else answered the slave breaker's cries for assistance. He struggled to subdue Frederick, but the slave deflected Covey's blows and clutched his attacker's throat with such force that his fingers drew blood. When Covey reached for a club, Frederick snatched him up and threw him into a pile of cow dung. After two hours, Covey, blood dripping from his wounds, broke loose and fled to his house, muttering threats at the defiant youngster.

Covey's retreat amazed Frederick. Striking a white man could have meant Frederick's death, but if Covey filed charges against

Unable to endure the torments of slave breaker Edward Covey, Douglass fled his confines. When he returned two days later, Covey was unable to subdue the unruly slave who had tasted freedom.

the rebellious lad his reputation as a slave breaker would be ruined. Covey had to keep Frederick's victory a secret. Never again would the slave breaker torment Frederick. Never again would Frederick consider himself a slave regardless of his legal condition. In his autobiography, he described his transformation:

> This battle with Mr. Covey . . . was the turning-point in my "life as a slave." It rekindled in my breast the smouldering embers of liberty . . . and revived a sense of my own manhood. . . . I was *nothing* before; *I was a man* now.[20]

A Free Man

By 1838, Frederick returned to Baltimore to work for Hugh Auld. In return for part of his wages, his master agreed to let him hire out as a skilled ship caulker. The arrangement gave Frederick considerable freedom. As long as Frederick paid his own expenses and gave Auld three dollars each week, he could come and go much as he pleased.

He also learned that increased liberty could mean increased risks. One day, four white workers, angry about working with a black man, beat Frederick severely. Despite the odds, he fought back.

Inside this slave's bruised, bloody body lived the soul of a free man. His job as a caulker left him time for a social life. While in Baltimore, Frederick met educated black men, men who served as proof that blacks could make their own way in the world. He also met Anna Murray, a free woman whose parents had been slaves. They fell in love. Frederick's love for Anna intensified his desire for freedom.

Hugh Auld saw the growing desire for independence in his handsome young slave and it made him suspicious. When Frederick arrived a day late with Auld's share of his weekly wages, the two nearly came to blows. Auld threatened not to allow him to hire out. At age twenty-one, Frederick decided it was time to follow the North Star.

Before escaping to the North, Douglass borrowed freedom papers, similar to this one, which alleged that he had been freed legally.

Bound for New York City

At great personal risk, one of his friends, a free black sailor, loaned Frederick a suit of clothes and his freedom papers. In Baltimore, Frederick boarded a train bound for New York City. On the trip he saw two of his former employers and feared they would identify him as a runaway. Neither recognized him. On September 4, 1838, Frederick stepped off the train in New York City.

He soon learned the meaning of freedom. An economic depression gripped New York and few wanted to hire a black man. A fugitive in a strange land, Frederick wandered the streets until he neared starvation. Fortunately, he learned about David Ruggles, a black man who was an officer on the New York Vigilance Committee, an organization that often aided runaways. Ruggles took the frightened runaway into his home. Within a few days, Anna came north and married Frederick.

Thinking Frederick could more easily find work in New England, Ruggles gave the newlyweds some money and put them on the train for New Bedford, Massachusetts. There a well-to-do black gave the couple lodging while Frederick sought work. Realizing that a runaway could not safely use his real name, at his host's suggestion Frederick adopted Douglass as a last name. Ironically, the name came from a novel by Sir Walter Scott, a writer popular among the southern planters whose way of life Douglass would help destroy.

Douglass Joins the Antislavery Movement

The newlyweds struggled to earn a living, Frederick working at manual labor jobs and Anna taking in laundry. Douglass also joined a black Methodist congregation because the mixed race congregations segregated blacks and whites. And with the pennies he could spare he subscribed to William Lloyd Garrison's *The Liberator*. He also began to attend antislavery meetings in New Bedford, quickly rising to positions of leadership.

In August 1841, William Lloyd Garrison met Douglass at a meeting of New Bedford's antislavery society. Garrison noted Douglass's noble bearing and powers of self-expression. Douglass was so moved by Garrison's passion for the cause of freedom that he decided to accompany a group of white and black abolitionists to a convention in Nantucket. The trip reminded him that the black man's problems in America went beyond slavery. When they boarded the steamboat for Nantucket, the captain insisted the whites and blacks be separated. After the group protested, the captain permitted the abolitionists to occupy the upper deck away from the other passengers.

After gaining his freedom, Douglass joined an antislavery society and began lecturing about his experiences as a slave.

With this insult fresh in his mind, Douglass suddenly found himself forced into the limelight. At the convention the next day, he was called on to address the audience. When he hesitantly spoke of his slave experiences, the crowd, and William Lloyd Garrison, responded enthusiastically. In his biography, *Frederick Douglass*, historian Philip S. Foner described the scene:

Greatly stirred, Garrison followed with an exciting address. . . . He asked the audience, "Have we been listening
to a thing, a piece of property, or to a man?" "A man! A
man!" came from five hundred voices. Then he asked if they
would ever allow Douglass to be carried back to slavery and
received a thunderous "No!" in reply.[21]

Douglass had caught the public eye at a critical moment in the
fight against slavery. Stung by intensifying abolitionist attacks on
slavery, southern planters insisted that God in his wisdom had
made blacks slaves because they were incapable of taking care of
themselves. In 1835, South Carolina Governor George McDuffie
proclaimed the new defense in a speech to his state legislature:

No human institution . . . is more manifestly consistent
with the will of God than domestic slavery. . . . [Blacks]
have all the qualities that fit them for slaves, and not
one . . . that would fit them to be freemen. . . . [it would]
be in vain to attempt . . . to make freemen of those whom
God has doomed to be slaves.[22]

Garrison realized that if whites considered blacks inferior they
probably would oppose emancipation. The abolitionists needed
bright, articulate blacks, preferably runaways, to convince whites
that people of African heritage were as capable as whites. Physically impressive, noble in bearing, eloquent, self-educated, and a
Christian man, Douglass was living proof of black competence.
Douglass provided Garrison the perfect spokesperson.

On the Lecture Circuit

On the strength of his Nantucket speech, the Massachusetts Anti-
Slavery Society offered to employ him as a paid lecturer. The
self-educated Douglass doubted he could handle the job. Yet here
was his chance to strike at slavery. Despite his doubts, Douglass
accepted and went on a lecture tour of New England fully expecting to be out of a job in three months.

He quickly proved equal to the task. With each speech, his
power to inspire the audience grew. Douglass had lived slavery. He
spoke of his experiences as a slave, of his separation from his family, of his unknown father and the mother he scarcely knew. His
account of the battle with Covey the slave breaker mesmerized audiences. How could a man who valued liberty over his own life be
unfit for freedom?

Douglass's travels on the lecture circuit provided him with daily
examples of the burdens racism put on whites to enforce an unjust

social system. When Douglass and his white associates boarded trains, conductors sometimes required him to sit in a car reserved for blacks. If Douglass resisted, and he often did, the conductors moved him by force. To their credit, Douglass's white companions usually accompanied him to the black accommodations. Perhaps these experiences helped Douglass realize that ultimately real freedom would mean racial equality, not just emancipation.

A Lecturer and a Publisher

As Douglass's reputation continued to grow, the American Anti-Slavery Society employed him as a lecturer. In 1845, he published a short autobiography entitled *Narrative of the Life of Frederick Douglass*, a powerful work that gained him national attention and provided him additional income. In the fall of that year, Douglass traveled to England.

In 1833, England had begun gradually freeing slaves throughout its empire, and black abolitionists enjoyed huge popularity there. The trip proved a triumph for Douglass.

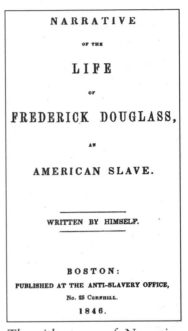

The title page of Narrative of the Life of Frederick Douglass, an American Slave *—the autobiography that gained Douglass international notoriety.*

His book sold enough copies to pay most of his expenses. English abolitionists also raised £150 to purchase Douglass's freedom. Now legally a free man he enjoyed a security he had never known before.

Douglass remained in England for two years enjoying his celebrity status. He might happily have stayed longer but conscience called him back to the battle against American slavery. By now Douglass believed he could reach a much wider audience through the printed word. Publishing his own antislavery periodical would also spare him the strain and risk of the lecture circuit. Only a few poorly produced black antislavery papers existed in the United States. His would fill the void.

Much to his surprise, Garrison and his other white abolitionist friends warned Douglass that his youth, lack of formal education, and lack of money would doom the project. Douglass suspected Garrison feared a new paper might lure black subscribers away from *The Liberator*. He had already begun to doubt the wisdom of Garrison's refusal to fight slavery either through force or political means. The time had come to act alone. At the end of 1847, with financial aid from English supporters, Douglass moved his family to Rochester, New York, and began publication of his paper. He named it *The North Star* for that bright light God had placed in the heavens to show the way to freedom.

Despite Garrison's objections, it soon became clear that Douglass had made some shrewd choices. Antislavery feeling ran high in Rochester. The city also boasted an active women's antislavery group. Its membership included Elizabeth Cady Stanton, Sojourner Truth, and Susan B. Anthony, some of the most famous antislavery activists of their time. Perhaps as important, the move to Rochester symbolized Douglass's growing independence from Garrison. Not only had he launched the paper without Garrison's blessing, he now was geographically separated from his old mentor. His success or failure would be his own.

Douglass lectures to an English audience. During Douglass's two-year visit to England, English abolitionists raised enough money to legally purchase his freedom.

Favorable Reviews

The project began so well that even the skeptical Garrison gave *The North Star* favorable reviews. Although the paper earned praise in the abolitionist community and attracted many new subscribers, it lost money. Douglass returned to the lecture circuit to raise funds for the publication and mortgaged his house to meet its expenses.

The paper quickly became a powerful voice appealing to the American conscience. In it Douglass addressed moral issues beyond slavery and equality. In 1848, Douglass questioned America's right to seize land conquered in its war with Mexico. Like other abolitionists, Douglass recognized that new territory could be used to add new slave states. He also considered the conquest an act of theft. One month after Mexico signed the Treaty of Guadalupe Hidalgo and surrendered half its territory to the United States, he used the pages of *The North Star* to shame Americans for their greed:

> In our judgment, those who have all along been loudly in favor of a vigorous prosecution of the war, and heralding its bloody triumphs . . . have no sincere love of peace, and are . . . rejoicing over . . . plunder. They have succeeded in robbing Mexico of her territory. . . . [We ought to] blush and hang our heads for shame . . . and crave pardon for our crimes at the hands of . . . God.[23]

Douglass Turns to Political Action

While the range of Douglass's moral concerns grew, he still focused on abolitionism. Douglass read extensively in political philosophy and history. He also consulted other abolitionists, often arguing about the best method to end slavery. Among them was Gerrit Smith of Rochester, a wealthy abolitionist who believed political action could end slavery. He also met one of Smith's friends, an odd character named John Brown.

When he met Brown in 1847, Douglass thought it remarkable that a white man should hold such passionate antislavery views. The men developed a lasting friendship. Douglass later revealed that Brown told him slavery was so evil that violence against slaveholders was justified. The argument touched something in Douglass. He had long accepted Garrison's view that it was every American's duty not to take part in politics since the Constitution recognized slavery. He also believed the struggle against slavery must be nonviolent, a strange attitude for the man who beat Covey the slave breaker.

Susan B. Anthony, the famous women's rights activist, was also a member of a prominent women's antislavery group located in Rochester, New York.

Like Garrison, Douglass had also believed the free states must separate from the slave-holding states. However, prospect of slavery expanding westward led him to support congressional passage of the Wilmot Proviso. The proviso would have forbidden slavery in the new territories annexed from Mexico. Douglass's support of the proviso indicated his growing belief that abolitionists should become politically active. He concluded that small political anti-slavery groups would one day become powerful enough to end slavery. Still a follower of Garrison, Douglass attended conventions of the Liberty Party and the Free Soil Party in 1848. Douglass saw the antislavery struggle's future more clearly than Garrison, but his old teacher bitterly attacked him for straying from the true abolitionist faith. By 1853, Douglass's support for political action to end slavery had ended their relationship. Douglass's change of heart came just as the antislavery battle reached critical mass.

In 1854, the Kansas-Nebraska Act repealed the Missouri Compromise, opened the possibility of new slave states, and triggered a storm of debate. Battles erupted between pro- and antislavery forces in the Kansas Territory. "Bleeding Kansas," as it became known, foretold the coming Civil War.

Formation of the Republican Party

Each side in the dispute over slavery argued its position more intensely than ever. The threat of an ever-expanding slave power drove many old Liberty Party members and Free Soilers, antislavery Whigs and Democrats to unite. In the summer of 1854 they formed the Republican Party. While the party did not seek an immediate end to slavery, it opposed spreading slavery to the territories. However timid its platform, in 1856 Douglass publicly supported the party's nomination of John C. Fremont for president. The instrument that would destroy slavery had been formed.

Infamous abolitionist John Brown impressed Douglass with his passion for the antislavery cause.

John Brown did not wait for the political process to end slavery. Late in October 1859, word of Brown's botched raid on the federal arsenal at Harper's Ferry, Virginia, reached Douglass. Incredibly, Old Brown had allowed letters discussing his plot to fall into the authorities' hands. Douglass's name, along with Gerrit Smith's and

A peace convention at Fort Scott, Kansas, turns violent as slavery opponents and supporters argue whether Kansas will be a free or slave state.

other prominent abolitionists, emerged from the documents. Virginia governor Henry Wise wanted Douglass arrested for his part in the conspiracy, and a Virginia court would surely have convicted and executed Douglass on the strength of Brown's letters. Some southerners had already offered rewards for the capture of Brown's associates. Facing abduction by bounty hunters or arrest by federal agents, Douglass fled to Canada. Within a few weeks he sailed for England. When Douglass returned to Rochester the following spring, the United States lay on the brink of civil war.

Douglass and the Civil War

For years, Douglass had warned that slavery must end before all Americans could truly be free. This, combined with his insistence that slaves were justified in both fleeing and fighting their masters made many whites see him as a dangerous agitator. In November 1860, Abraham Lincoln's election to the presidency sparked the conflict Douglass had long said was unavoidable. Hardly an abolitionist in the sense that Douglass and Garrison were, Lincoln intended only to stop the further spread of slavery. He even laid plans for emancipation taking place over a generation, with masters receiving payment for their slaves. Even this proved too much for white southerners. They preferred secession and war to life under Lincoln.

Although President Lincoln declared the North only took up arms to restore the Union and not to free slaves, Douglass understood that northern victory would end slavery. Douglass knew blacks North and South rising to the call of freedom could prove critical to Union victory. In speeches and articles for his publication, now called *Frederick Douglass' Paper*, he called for freedom for all slaves and recruitment of black soldiers.

Although blacks had served ably in America's wars, many northern whites, remembering Nat Turner's murderous rampage, flinched at the thought of armed black men. When thousands of blacks volunteered for military service, the army rejected them. Even worse, as the Union army advanced southward, it returned runaway slaves to their masters.

A Step Toward Abolition

Despite this, Douglass believed that the need for recruits after the long string of defeats the Union suffered in the war's first two years would force northern acceptance of black soldiers. Douglass believed black military service would hasten emancipation, but Lincoln displayed little interest in abolition or black troops. In August 1862, he told an audience of free blacks they

Douglass encouraged blacks to enlist in the Union army, believing their involvement would help secure a northern victory and hasten emancipation.

should establish colonies in other countries. Douglass fumed that even the war had failed to break slavery's hold on the country. The day of freedom lay closer than Douglass realized. After a narrow Union victory in September 1862, at the Battle of Antietam, Lincoln issued his Emancipation Proclamation. Although the proclamation left many slaves in bondage, Douglass rejoiced that the United States had taken a decisive step toward abolition. Shortly afterward, the War Department cleared the way for enlisting black soldiers into the army. For months, runaway slaves in areas occupied by the Union army had been enrolled for limited duty. Now Massachussets governor John A. Andrews began enlisting blacks from all across the North for military service.

Douglass recruited thousands to the cause. Military service, he declared, gave blacks a chance to prove their worth to skeptical whites. Douglass argued that blacks could never truly be free until they had learned to use weapons in defense of their liberty. Two of his sons answered the call. In May 1863, he watched as the 54th Massachusetts Regiment, the first all-black regiment bound for combat, paraded through Boston. In the same city where American patriots had once taken up arms against British oppression, Douglass saw black men marching to free their brothers and sisters.

For the remainder of the war, Douglass suspended publication of his paper and continued to travel, recruiting black soldiers. In the summer of 1863 he met with President Lincoln, asking him to guarantee equal treatment to black soldiers, especially in pay and promotion. While other abolitionists considered their work done, Douglass realized that slavery would not truly end until black Americans enjoyed full equality and citizenship.

The Quest for Citizenship and Equality

By the time Confederate General Robert E. Lee surrendered at Appomattox Courthouse in April 1865, several slave states had already abolished slavery. Ratification of the thirteenth amendment to the Constitution soon ended slavery in the rest. At the American

Black infantrymen pose for a photograph in 1862. During the Civil War Douglass traveled across the country recruiting black soldiers.

Anti-Slavery Society convention in May 1865, Garrison proposed dissolving the organization since its work was done. With a passionate appeal Douglass persuaded the delegates to keep the organization alive lest white southerners find new ways to oppress blacks.

He even urged President Andrew Johnson to support full citizenship and voting rights for blacks, but Johnson received the idea cooly. While most southern states were under the Union army's control and unable to vote, Congress proposed the fourteenth and fifteenth amendments to the United States Constitution. Anxious to keep old rebels from regaining power, Congress required the former Confederate states to ratify the amendments to gain readmission to the Union. In July 1868, Secretary of State William Seward declared the Fourteenth Amendment granting blacks citizenship in force. Then in March 1870, the Fifteenth Amendment granting blacks the vote became part of the Constitution.

In only five years, Douglass had seen blacks legally transformed from property into voting citizens. Now his people would have to throw off centuries of ignorance and oppression to enjoy their new status. Douglass knew many white southerners would place every possible obstacle in their paths. Former masters defrauded free blacks who sharecropped their land. Organizations such as the Ku Klux Klan terrorized the new citizens if they complained of mistreatment or cast their ballots for the Republican Party. The struggle for black liberty had only begun.

Blacks flock to a polling center during an election. The Fifteenth Amendment, passed in March 1870, granted blacks the right to vote.

Grateful citizens of Washington, D.C., pay their respects to Frederick Douglass, the unfailing defender of black freedom.

Still, both Douglass and the cause he championed had made huge strides. Now the most respected black man in America, the former runaway was appointed to important federal positions including marshal, recorder of deeds for the District of Columbia, and finally, in 1889, United States consul general to Haiti. None of these tasks distracted Douglass from the defense of black freedom. Leaving his diplomatic post in Haiti in 1891, he found an America cursed by new attempts to deny blacks the vote. New state laws required citizens to pay poll taxes or pass literacy tests before voting. This threatened poor blacks and whites alike. Southern states also imposed "grandfather clauses" denying the vote to citizens whose ancestors could not vote. More ominously, blacks increasingly died in lynchings.

His zeal for the cause undimmed by age, he traveled, condemning these newest outrages in fiery speeches and articles. The pace proved too much for the old activist. In February 1895, after delivering a speech, he collapsed in his home and died. Americans black and white, rich and poor mourned the loss of the runaway who had twice fled his country to save his life. In Rochester, thousands turned out to view his coffin. This restless man who had laid the foundation of black freedom was laid to rest. New generations of men and women would build on his work.

CHAPTER 5

Harriet Tubman: Black Moses

As Frederick Douglass's masters had learned, Maryland was a difficult place to keep slaves. Bordered by Pennsylvania, a nonslave state, freedom lay tantalizingly close. Ben and Old Rit Ross's daughter Araminta was born within reach of that temptation, in Dorchester County, Maryland, on the plantation of Edward Brodas. As usual, little Araminta's birth date wasn't written down since Ben and Rit could not read or write. Harriet, as the baby would later be called, probably arrived in 1820.

Ben and Rit welcomed this little girl into their already large family, but to slaves childbirth was a mixed blessing. While both black and white farm children died often enough from disease and accidents, slave children could be sold and taken away from their parents. In hard economic times, Maryland planters often raised money by selling some of their slaves or hiring them out for wages.

Harriet's Early Training

When Harriet was perhaps seven or eight years old, her master hired her to the wife of James Cook. Mrs. Cook, a weaver, wanted the little girl to help with her work. Accustomed to following her father as he cut timber in the woods, Harriet displayed little talent or desire to help with the weaving. Anxious to make the little hired girl useful, Mrs. Cook sent her to work with her husband, a trapper. This suited Harriet far better. Here she continued to learn the ways of the wild as she had with her father. Harriet's knowledge of woodcraft would prove far more important than she could ever dream.

The little girl's work as a trapper's assistant was cut short by illness. Harriet waded cold streams tending the traps and became so sick with bronchitis that her employers returned her to Old Rit's care. Old Rit's herbal remedies restored Harriet's health, but the episode had lasting effects. Harriet believed the sickness changed the tone of her voice. Years later, listeners marveled at her unique speaking and singing voice, deepened forever by sickness.

A slave family performs chores in front of its meager cabin. Harriet Tubman, the woman who would become the savior of her people, spent her childhood on a similar plantation in Maryland.

Her health restored, Harriet returned to the Cook home. Her second stay proved no more successful than the first. Mrs. Cook soon sent Harriet back to the Brodas plantation complaining that the little girl was hopelessly stupid. Brodas could not afford idle slaves on his plantation. She soon found herself hired out again, this time to a couple with a baby. Harriet's new mistress required her to perform household chores by day and tend to the baby by night. With no training as a maid or a nurse, the girl had no idea how to perform her duties and constantly angered her mistress. After a full day's work, at night Harriet rocked the baby's cradle to keep it quiet. Exhausted, she often nodded off, and the child, accustomed to constant attention, would cry, awakening its parents. Whenever this happened, the mistress would whip Harriet on her back and neck, sometimes leaving open wounds. Night after night the abuse continued. Harriet learned to sleep while remaining alert to sounds of the baby stirring or of her mistress's approach. Still, the child sometimes cried, and each time Harriet felt the bite of the lash.

Slaves harvest cotton on their master's plantation. Tubman excelled at such manual labor, impressing those around her with her physical strength.

Once the mistress, seeing Harriet steal a lump of sugar, whipped her severely. At the end of her endurance, the girl finally fled with her tormentor in hot pursuit. Harriet ran until her mistress gave up the chase. Safe for the moment, the little fugitive hid in a hog pen. Frightened and desperate for food, she spent four days concealed there eating food intended for the animals. She knew capture would mean a severe beating, but misery and hunger drove her back to her mistress.

The incident ended her employment. Once again, Harriet found herself returned to the Brodas plantation, her mistress complaining that she was stupid and unreliable. Little Harriet's value as a slave was dropping rapidly. Finally, Brodas hired her out as a field worker. Here she excelled. Her remarkable strength amazed both her masters and her fellow slaves. She easily carried loads that would have strained grown men. Now more contented, Harriet grew into young womanhood. Day after day, she went to the fields, singing the hymns she loved as she labored.

Despite her gift for manual labor, Harriet's defiant spirit caused her trouble. When she was thirteen, Harriet saw a male slave escape. When the overseer gave chase, Harriet stepped into his path. The overseer threw a two-pound weight at the runaway, missed and smashed Harriet's forehead leaving her unconscious. Old Rit took her home and nursed her daughter from Christmas until the following March. When she finally felt well enough to venture outside her parents' cabin, she suffered severe headaches. Thereafter, she would suddenly fall into a deep sleep at unpredictable times.

Fear Leads to Flight

Tubman's defiance toward the overseer had exhausted Brodas's patience. He decided to sell her, but potential buyers balked once they saw the scars on her back and head. These were the marks of a troublesome slave. Tubman knew her master intended to sell her and two of her brothers. Frightened and angry she prayed that God might strike Brodas down. Soon the word reached the slave quarters that the master was gravely ill. Not long afterwards, Brodas died.

Tubman felt deep guilt. She had prayed for a man's death, and now he lay beyond the help of her prayers. Years later, Sarah Bradford wrote Tubman's account of the story. "He died just as he had lived," she told Bradford in her thick dialect,

> a wicked, bad man. Oh, den it 'peared like I would give de world full of silver and gold, if I had it, to bring dat pore soul back, I would give *myself*; I would give eberyting! But he was gone, I couldn't pray for him no more.[24]

Always a devout Christian, Tubman's faith intensified after her near death and her master's passing. As the scriptures required, she prayed without ceasing. "Pears like I prayed all de time," she said:

> I was always talking to de Lord. When I went to the horse-trough to wash my face, and took up de water in my hands, I said, "Oh, Lord, wash me, make me clean." When I took up de towel to wipe my face and hands, I cried, "Oh, Lord, for Jesus' sake, wipe away all my sins!"[25]

While Tubman prayed for her spirit to be cleansed she still feared her body would be sold. Word passed quickly among the slaves that Brodas's will required no slaves be sold outside Maryland. That provided some comfort. Slaves considered being sold into the deep South a death sentence. Tubman knew such promises meant little. Long ago Brodas had promised to free Old Rit but had never done so. Brodas's son now inherited the estate. Too young to manage his own affairs, that task fell to a man known as Doc Thompson.

At first things went well under Thompson. He hired Tubman and Ben to a builder named John Stewart. At first assigned housework, Tubman asked Stewart to send her outside to work with her father. He agreed and soon discovered this thin little woman could do a man's work in the field behind a plow or in the woods with an axe. Tubman cherished time spent in the woods with Ben. There she sharpened her knowledge of plants, especially medicinal herbs. Ben also taught her to move noiselessly through the woods.

While working for Stewart, she fell in love with and married John Tubman, a free black man. John told Tubman his parents had been slaves but were freed when their master died. This news reminded Tubman that Old Rit had once been promised her freedom. With the few dollars she had saved, she hired an attorney to investigate her mother's legal status. The attorney found that one of Old Rit's former owners had agreed to free her but died before acting on the promise. Since then, Old Rit had been sold and resold.

Dreaming of Freedom

The information troubled Tubman. Too often, masters conveniently forgot their promises. Two of her sisters had already been sold into the South. Now she feared Doc Thompson might sell her away from her beloved John. At night she dreamed of the chain gangs coming to the slave quarters and rounding up the slaves. Over and over again she dreamed she was flying north, high above the fields and farms. In the dream she would near a fence or a river and would see a white woman welcoming her with outstretched arms to the land of freedom.

Eventually, she told John she might run away. To Tubman's amazement, John warned her that he would alert the master if she at-

Increasingly frustrated with slave life and fearing she would be sold into the South, Tubman plotted her escape without her husband's knowledge.

tempted to escape. Clearly, John no longer trusted her and she could no longer trust him. Still Tubman dreamed of freedom.

In 1849, when Edward Brodas's young heir died, Doc Thompson began selling the plantation's slaves into the deep South where they would fetch a higher price. Two of Tubman's sisters were

$200 Reward.

RANAWAY from the subscriber, on the night of Thursday, the 30th of Sepember,

FIVE NEGRO SLAVES,

To-wit : one Negro man, his wife, and three children.

The man is a black negro, full height, very erect, his face a little thin. He is about forty years of age, and calls himself *Washington Reed*, and is known by the name of Washington. He is probably well dressed, possibly takes with him an ivory headed cane, and is of good address. Several of his teeth are gone.

Mary, his wife, is about thirty years of age, a bright mulatto woman, and quite stout and strong.

The oldest of the children is a boy, of the name of FIELDING, twelve years of age, a dark mulatto, with heavy eyelids. He probably wore a new cloth cap.

MATILDA, the second child, is a girl, six years of age, rather a dark mulatto, but a bright and smart looking child.

MALCOLM, the youngest, is a boy, four years old, a lighter mulatto than the last, and about equally as bright. He probably also wore a cloth cap. If examined, he will be found to have a swelling at the navel.

Washington and Mary have lived at or near St. Louis, with the subscriber, for about 15 years.

It is supposed that they are making their way to Chicago, and that a white man accompanies them, that they will travel chiefly at night, and most probably in a covered wagon.

A reward of $150 will be paid for their apprehension, so that I can get them, if taken within one hundred miles of St. Louis, and $200 if taken beyond that, and secured so that I can get them, and other reasonable additional charges, if delivered to the subscriber, or to THOMAS ALLEN, Esq., at St. Louis, Mo. The above negroes, for the last few years, have been in possession of Thomas Allen, Esq., of St. Louis.

WM. RUSSELL.

ST. LOUIS, Oct. 1, 1847.

A broadside offers a reward for the apprehension of a runaway slave family. Such notices were common in slaveholding states and hindered a slave's ability to escape.

among the first to go, shackled into the chain gang. Whether John approved or not, she resolved to escape.

On her first attempt, Tubman led three of her brothers northward through the darkness with her. Soon tired and frightened, the three men forced Tubman to return to the plantation with them. Her first attempt had failed. Next time she would have to go alone, but she would not be without friends. Once a white woman who lived in the neighborhood had seen Tubman working in the fields and stopped to chat. Before she left, the woman told Tubman to come to her if she ever needed help. She would need help soon.

One day Tubman heard that Doc Thompson intended to send her south with a Georgia slave buyer. That night she wrapped a small supply of food in a cloth and slipped out of her cabin while John slept. As Tubman stepped into the cool night air fear crept into her heart. What if the master saw her away from the slave quarters? What if she fell into one of her sleeping spells when she most needed to remain alert? With a soft prayer asking God to sustain her, she turned her back on her home.

Slaves escape to the North on the Underground Railroad—the network of abolitionists who fostered fugitive slaves and helped them gain freedom.

Soon she arrived at the doorstep of the woman who had offered help. A few taps on the door brought the white woman to the threshold. Showing no signs of surprise, the woman gave Tubman a piece of paper with two names on it and gave her directions to another house. Tubman had just made her first stop on the Underground Railroad.

That night she passed safely through the woods to the next house. Each stop along this secret network led to another. At one house her host had her do yard work in broad daylight. After all, a black woman doing chores would not arouse suspicion. One farmer transported her concealed in a load of produce. All sorts of people helped her—free blacks, Quakers, farmers who spoke with German accents. Tubman knew Doc Thompson surely had alerted the countryside about her disappearance. Any of these strangers could have returned her to Thompson and claimed a reward. None did. Ninety miles later, Harriet Tubman stepped onto Pennsylvania's free soil.

She looked at herself to see if she had changed now that she was no longer someone else's property. At first Pennsylvania looked like heaven, but loneliness swept over her. She had escaped, but her family remained behind in bondage. "I was free," she later said,

> but dere was no one to welcome me to de land of freedom, I was a stranger in a strange land, and my home . . . was down in de old cabin quarter, wid de ole folks, and my brudders and sisters. But to dis solemn resolution I came; I was free, and dey should be free also. I would make a

home for dem in de North, and de Lord helping me, I would bring dem all dere.[26]

A Conductor on the Underground Railroad

First she had to make a living. In Philadelphia, she found work cleaning houses and doing other domestic chores. Every dime she saved would finance her return to Dorchester County. She talked to other fugitives who had made the trip north. She went to the Philadelphia Vigilance Committee, which aided runaways. The information she gathered, coupled with her own experiences, gave her a broader view of the Underground Railroad. Clearly, if she had reached Pennsylvania without any knowledge of the system, fugitives escaping with a guide would almost certainly succeed—as long as they did not turn back. Tubman would see to it that none turned back.

In 1850, Tubman learned that her sister and her two children were about to be sold into the deep South. Her brother-in-law, a free black man named John Bowley, spirited his family away from the slave pens with the help of a Quaker conductor on the Underground Railroad. Despite the risks, Tubman insisted on meeting the family and guiding them at least part of the way to Philadelphia where she deposited them in the hands of the Vigilance Committee. For the moment, they were safe, but the danger to all blacks in the North had just increased. Congress had passed the new Fugitive Slave Law that required all law enforcement officials to return runaways to their owners. Aided by the new law, southern slaveholders pursued their runaways northward.

Ignoring the increased risk, Tubman continued her trips to Maryland. Whenever she had saved enough money, she returned to the old plantation and freed a few more members of her family. Once she attempted to persuade her husband to go north with her but found him living with another woman and determined to stay in Dorchester County. After this she guided runaways who were not related to her. Slaves with the scent of freedom in their nostrils knew when to expect her. The masters never seemed to know. They only heard rumors that someone the slaves now called "Moses" was stealing their property. Like the ancient biblical hero, Tubman had become God's instrument to lead her people to freedom.

Because of the new Fugitive Slave Law, the promised land was farther away than ever. Tubman began to guide her passengers all the way to Canada. Once there, United States law could no longer touch a fugitive. On these long trips some of Tubman's passengers gave up and insisted on returning to their masters. Those who did found themselves facing Tubman's Colt revolver. Tubman realized a returning slave might betray the Underground Railroad to a white master and permitted no one to turn back. According to biographer Sarah Bradford,

> Often the men who followed her would give out, and footsore, and bleeding, they would drop on the ground, groaning that they could not take another step. . . . Then the revolver carried by this . . . daring pioneer, would come out, while pointing it at their heads she would say, "Dead [men] tell no tales; you go on or die!" And by this heroic treatment she compelled them to drag their weary limbs along on their northward journey.[27]

The little woman once rejected as hopelessly stupid displayed cunning and courage during her Maryland forays. Sometimes she drugged small children to keep them quiet when enemies were near. Often she disguised herself when returning to Maryland. Once, dressed as an old woman, she strolled through her home county in broad daylight carrying two live chickens. Seeing a former employer approaching, she lowered her head so her sunbonnet shaded her face. Then she shook the chickens so they flapped their wings and distracted the man. She passed him unrecognized.

Law enforcement officials capture a runaway slave. The Fugitive Slave Law mandated that runaways were to be returned to their legal owners.

On another occasion, Tubman led a party of runaways to a house on the Underground Railroad but found a hostile stranger there who sent them away. Tubman assumed the stranger would send the authorities to capture them and quickly hid her people in the tall grass of a swamp. There they spent the day, wet, cold, and hungry, fearing discovery at any moment. After hours in hiding, they saw a stranger dressed in Quaker clothing strolling along the edge of the swamp. Without looking aside, in a soft voice he said his horse and wagon stood in the barnyard of the next farm. The man repeated the message over and over as he walked out of sight. Tubman led her party out of hiding and found the wagon ready and provisioned with food as the man had said. After transporting her people to the next safe house, she left the wagon and horse with a man she trusted to return it.

Tubman displayed incredible courage and determination while a conductor on the Underground Railroad.

A Symbol of Freedom

In all her exploits, Tubman displayed confidence people of lesser faith could scarcely understand. Moses had become a legend in Maryland, and slave owners watched for her return. Together they offered rewards as high as $40,000 for her capture, and if captured she could expect worse than whipping or re-enslavement. Now a symbol of freedom known to both blacks and whites, capture meant death.

Tubman continued her work. She escorted some runaways as far as St. Catherines, Canada. There she helped escaped slaves find work and establish homes. Sometimes she helped them through hard times by getting contributions from abolitionists or paying their expenses out of her own pocket. St. Catherines had become a refuge for runaways, and Tubman made it her winter home. Still she regularly returned to Maryland, finally guiding several of her brothers and her parents to freedom. Tubman bought a small house in Auburn and settled her parents there. In all she made nineteen trips south and led over three hundred people out of bondage.

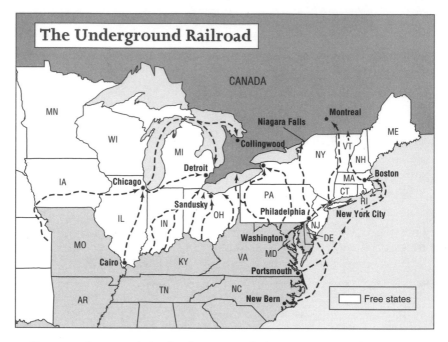

The Underground Railroad

CANADA

MN

WI

MI

Detroit

Chicago

IA

IL

IN

OH

Sandusky

Cairo

MO

KY

TN

AR

NC

New Bern

VA

MD

Washington

Portsmouth

DE

NJ

Philadelphia

PA

NY

New York City

CT

RI

MA

Boston

NH

VT

ME

Montreal

Niagara Falls

Collingwood

☐ Free states

By now her exploits had attracted the attention of some anti-slavery activists. In the winter of 1858–59, she met Franklin B. Sanborn, a wealthy abolitionist, in Boston. Sanborn asked Tubman to speak at antislavery rallies. Sanborn convinced her that through speaking she could strike a powerful blow for freedom. She agreed to make the speeches.

At first this small, plain-speaking black woman seemed out of place in front of elegant, educated white audiences. She shared the speaker's platform with abolitionist giants such as Wendell Phillips, a member of one of Boston's wealthiest and most respected families. Sometimes Tubman lapsed into one of her deep sleeps while sitting on the platform, but when this battered little woman told her stories and sang her hymns, audiences forgot everything else. The lecture circuit made Tubman a celebrity. Tubman helped destroy the proslavery myth that blacks were happier as slaves than as free people. When she spoke, white audiences heard a woman who fled slavery and continued to risk her freedom and her life leading others from bondage.

John Brown

Still, some abolitionists wanted to attack slavery on a grander, more violent scale. In the winter of 1857 and 1858, Tubman had experienced a recurring dream. In the dream, she saw a snake whose face took the face of a man, an old man with a white beard and intense blue-gray eyes. The bearded man wanted to speak to her but could not and was struck down by a swarm of men. The dream troubled Tubman until one day she met the man with the blue-gray eyes—John Brown. Introduced to Tubman by a mutual friend, Brown described his plan to make safe havens for escaped slaves in the South. There he and a small army of his followers would arm them to resist recapture. With this in mind, he asked Tubman to tell him the hiding places she had used during her trips south. Brown added that he wanted her to enlist blacks for his liberating army and to guide those he freed to Canada.

At first, Tubman hesitated. Such information could endanger countless people in the Underground Railroad. She also knew Brown's plan could lead to a bloodbath in the South. Eventually, Brown won her cooperation. He said he would contact her again later. Although he continued to speak of her as an ally in his correspondence, Tubman's role in Brown's scheme never materialized. On October 17, 1859, a feeling of doom swept over her. She told a friend that Brown was in trouble. Later that day, Tubman received news of Brown's capture during a raid on the federal arsenal at Harper's Ferry, Virginia.

Word of Brown's trial and execution the following month saddened her, but she soon realized that Brown's raid had moved the

Tubman (far left) poses with a group of blacks whom she helped escape from slavery. Her heroic deeds gained her the acclaim of both blacks and abolitionists.

freedom clock forward. While she had freed hundreds, the events he had set in motion would free millions.

Tubman Goes to War

By the spring of 1860, signs that the day of reckoning was coming appeared everywhere. The increasingly powerful Republican Party seemed certain to nominate an antislavery presidential candidate. Prominent white southerners openly spoke of breaking away from the United States if antislavery forces won the elections.

With tensions rising throughout the country, friends begged Tubman to remain in Canada beyond the reach of U.S. officials that might recapture her. Unafraid, Tubman made her last trip to Maryland, bringing a slave family to freedom. A few months after her return, the Civil War began. As northern armies entered the South, thousands of slaves fled their masters and sought refuge with Union troops.

Massachusetts governor John Andrew, a determined opponent of slavery, sent for Tubman and asked her to go south with the army and help deal with the refugees. In 1862, Tubman arrived in Port Royal, South Carolina, an area recently seized by Union troops. There she worked tirelessly in a hospital for contrabands (runaway slaves). Day and night she dressed wounds, administered herbal remedies, and comforted the sick. Giving up her privilege of drawing government rations since some of her patients resented it, she supported herself financially by baking pies and selling home-brewed root beer.

At times, Tubman served as a spy, slipping behind enemy lines. In June 1863, she accompanied a force of ex-slaves led by Colonel James Montgomery up the Combahee River. The raiders intended to clear enemy mines from the stream and to carry away as many contrabands as possible. As the Union gunboats steamed along the Combahee, hundreds of slaves flocked to the shores anxious to escape their masters. When troops sent rowboats to pick them up, many slaves nearly swamped the boats trying to board. At Montgomery's request, Tubman sang to the blacks. The soothing words of her song drifted across the river ending the panic. That day, the steamers carried nearly eight hundred people to freedom.

Tubman's Final Years

The war's end found her at Fortress Monroe in South Carolina. Her task had been accomplished. Her people were free. Tubman returned to a quiet life in Auburn, New York. For years afterward, her stories of the Underground Railroad and her adventures in the

Runaway slaves are photographed in a Union army camp. During the war thousands of contrabands flocked to the Union lines seeking refuge.

Civil War fascinated the townspeople. Still unable to repay the mortgage on her home, she petitioned the U.S. government requesting a pension for her services in the war. Despite letters from many influential men including Secretary of State William Seward, her request was denied.

Realizing her plight, a schoolteacher from Auburn interviewed her and wrote a short biography of Tubman called *Scenes in the Life of Harriet Tubman*. Its publication in 1869 brought Tubman enough income to repay the mortgage with money to spare. During the last years of her life, Tubman turned her house into a home for poor, elderly blacks. As always, Tubman found ways to use her tiny income for the benefit of others. Tubman died in March 1913. Few of the old abolitionists survived her. In July 1914, at a commemorative service, the people of Auburn dedicated a bronze plaque to Tubman's memory. Long before Tubman's death, Sarah Bradford envisioned her friend's entry into heaven:

> I . . . see a future day when the wrongs of earth will be righted, and justice, long delayed, will assert itself. I . . . see that our poor Tubman has passed within "one of dem gates," and has received the welcome, "Come, thou blessed of my Father. . . ."
>
> And as she stands in her modest way just within the celestial gate, I . . . see a kind hand laid upon her dark head, and . . . hear a gentle voice saying in her ear, "Friend, come up higher!"[28]

CHAPTER 6

Nat Turner: Preacher Turned Terrorist

The belief that they would go to heaven helped many slaves endure lives of hardship and toil. Most were laid to rest in unmarked graves and forgotten by generations to come. Not Nat Turner. His name struck cold fear into the hearts of white southerners long after his death. Seldom does a common farm worker have such impact on his world, but Nat Turner did. And he did it all in forty-eight hours.

Born the property of Benjamin Turner, owner of a small plantation in Southampton County, Virginia, Nat Turner enjoyed an easier life than slaves of the deep South. Neither the Virginia climate nor the labor required of Virginia slaves was particularly harsh. The Turner plantation's small size encouraged familiarity between whites and blacks. Nat's white master may have considered his black servants more like family than slaves. If so, he misjudged Nat Turner.

Early in life, Nat Turner displayed intelligence well beyond his fellow slaves. Even whites who later feared and hated him acknowledged his intellectual abilities. Turner recalled that when he was a very young child an adult put a book in his hands to keep him from crying. Much to everyone's surprise, little Nat identified the letters in the book. According to Turner, both whites and blacks thought the incident remarkable. He took every opportunity to build his reading skills, snatching a look at white children's schoolbooks whenever he could. By the time Turner reached adulthood, his fellow slaves considered him exceptionally clever. Some slaves, recognizing Turner's leadership qualities, asked him to help them plot petty thefts.

Whites also saw Turner as gifted. They noted Turner's devotion to Bible study and gave him opportunities to preach to other slaves. A compelling preacher, Turner truly seemed a godsend. Anxious to spread the gospel, whites in Southampton County permitted Turner to move freely, preaching as he went. Turner gained followers.

A black preacher conducts religious services on a plantation in 1863. Through his preaching, Nat Turner gained the respect of both blacks and whites.

Turner's Vision

He deliberately created an image of himself as a mystic. Turner avoided socializing with other slaves. Whenever time permitted, he prayed, fasted, and studied the Bible. Turner claimed one passage, Luke 12:31, especially interested him: "Seek ye the kingdom of God; and all . . . things shall be added unto you." He prayed daily for insight into the passage. Then one day while he was working in the field, he said, the verse's importance was revealed to him. Shortly before his death, Turner explained the experience in his own words:

> As I was praying one day at my plow, the Spirit spoke to me, saying "Seek ye the kingdom of Heaven and all things shall be added unto you. . . ." And I was greatly astonished and for two years prayed continually, whenever my duty would permit. And then again I had the same revelation, which fully confirmed me in the impression that I was ordained for some great purpose in the hands of the Almighty. . . .
>
> I began to direct my attention to this great object . . . for which . . . I felt I was intended. Knowing the influence I

had obtained over the minds of my fellow servants . . . I now began to prepare them for my purpose.[29]

Now Turner believed he understood why he was superior to other men. He was chosen by God.

At first, Turner's sense of mission seemed limited to the belief that he was too capable and intelligent to remain a slave. The solution seemed simple. Turner ran away. After hiding in a forest for a month, he willingly returned to his master. Turner believed that while he was in hiding, the Spirit had told him to return to his master and to seek God's kingdom, not his own selfish will. According to Turner, the Spirit revealed his destiny through a vision.

In the vision, Turner said he beheld a great struggle between blacks and whites—a racial Judgment Day.

> I saw white spirits and black spirits engaged in battle, and the sun was darkened, the thunder rolled in the heavens, and blood flowed in streams, and I heard a voice saying, "Such is your luck, such you are called to see, and let it come rough or smooth, you must surely bear it. . . ." After this revelation in the year 1825 . . . I sought more than ever to obtain true holiness before the great day of judgement should appear. . . . And from the first steps of righteousness until the last, was I made perfect.[30]

For the next three years Turner considered himself guided by the Holy Spirit. He became a preacher, delivering sermons to both blacks and whites. He immersed himself in the book of Revelation, the book of the Bible that speaks of the end of the world and Judgment Day. He believed he saw signs of the end times everywhere.

He beheld miracles large and small. Jesus appeared to him in the heavens, he said. He saw the dew formed as droplets of blood, the blood of the crucified savior shed upon the earth. A white neighbor whom he had told the end was near miraculously recovered from serious illness. Turner anxiously awaited God's call to action. Finally, in May 1828, he claimed he heard a loud noise in the sky followed by the voice of the Spirit telling him the Serpent was unleashed. He would see a sign in the heavens when he was to act. In February 1831, a solar eclipse darkened the east coast of the United States. The time had come.

The Insurrection

Turner recruited a handful of trusted slaves. By taking only a few men into his confidence he reduced the risks of betrayal and detection. Turner told his followers God called them to strike down their masters with their own weapons. Late night meetings took place in the cane brakes [thickets]. Conspirators gathered axes and other edged farm tools that could serve as weapons. On the night of August 20, 1831, Turner and his followers held a feast deep in the woods to celebrate the beginning of their enterprise. They devoured a roast pig, washed the meal down with brandy, and set to their work.

It was a Sunday night. Turner and six followers began at the home of Turner's master, Joseph Travis. Travis had bought Turner the year before, and Turner admitted his master treated him kindly. Kindness counted for little that night. To avoid alarming the neighborhood, one of the slaves climbed a ladder, crept into the house through a second-story window, and opened the front door. Quietly, the intruders gathered the firearms that they knew were in the house. The conspirators decided that as the group's leader Turner must strike the first blow. He agreed and with one of his men entered Travis's bedroom.

As his master lay sleeping, Turner struck him with a hatchet. Only wounded, Travis sprang from his bed and called for his wife. In an instant, Turner's partner killed the injured man with an axe and murdered Mrs. Travis as she lay in bed. After killing two more members of the Travis family, Turner and his men looted the house

Nat Turner (standing, left) confers with fellow conspirators during his 1831 uprising. Fifty-seven whites were brutally murdered during the revolt.

and left the building. Minutes after leaving, one of the conspirators realized they had left a baby alive in the house. Two of Turner's men returned and killed the child. From the beginning the slaves swore they would spare no one, man or woman, adult or child.

Their first attack had succeeded completely. At the Travis's the slaves had added muskets and ammunition to their armaments. More important, some of the plantation's slaves joined Turner. With obvious pride, Turner formed his recruits into military ranks and drilled them. Satisfied with their discipline, Turner marched his little command to the next farmhouse, the home of Salathul Francis. One of Francis's slaves awakened his master claiming to have brought him a letter. When Francis opened the door for his trusted servant, the slaves dragged him out and murdered him.

The quiet rural neighborhood of Southampton County proved a perfect killing ground for the slaves. Although country folks possessed weapons and knew how to use them, they did not fear attack. Slaves entered houses through unlocked doors. Slaves knew where to find weapons at each home. Masters usually trusted their slaves. In one instance, a conspirator saw his master standing in a field, beckoned to him, and killed him as he approached. It was as if the whites could not comprehend what was happening to them.

The March to Jerusalem

Within the first twenty-four hours, Turner's force had grown to sixty men, some on horseback. All carried axes, swords, clubs, or firearms. Up to now this large armed body had met no resistance, but while the slaves had killed almost every white in a twenty-mile area, survivors had escaped and spread the alarm. A white counterstrike was already underway. To make matters worse, many of Turner's men broke into their dead masters' liquor supplies and drank themselves senseless. Still, the black messiah intended to march his little army to the Southampton county seat. There the rebels expected to seize more weapons and supplies and to enlist more recruits. The town was called Jerusalem.

On the way to Jerusalem, Turner's band divided into smaller groups to attack several plantations. Turner and the remainder of his force stumbled across a group of white militia that had marched from Jerusalem to suppress the uprising. The whites unleashed a quick volley and then retreated toward a second body of militia that followed close behind them. Turner ordered his men to form ranks and return fire. Several whites fell wounded, but by this time the main force of militia appeared and blasted away at the blacks. Lead balls ripped through Turner's most trusted lieu-

Turner is finally captured after his murderous rampage. Like his fellow conspirators, Turner stood trial for his crimes and was quickly convicted.

tenants. Confusion reigned. Those blacks not killed or wounded fled. Joining in the flight, Turner planned to reform his forces and enter Jerusalem by another route.

By now Turner found armed whites almost everywhere. He returned to his old neighborhood to raise more recruits, but blundered into two more skirmishes with the whites. His remaining men panicked and fled. Now alone, Turner attempted to save himself. Reaching the Travis plantation, he gathered a supply of food and dug himself a hiding place under a pile of fence rails in a field. There, the man who believed himself to be God's avenging warrior hid for six weeks while the militia ran his followers to the ground.

Capture and Trial of the Rebels

The whites brutally crushed the revolt. Those of Turner's men not killed in the pursuit were captured, tried, and executed. As many as one hundred blacks were killed in the days following Turner's uprising. Some had aided Turner. Some had boldly expressed support for the rebels. Surprisingly, authorities saw to it that courts carefully followed proper legal procedures. Newspapers covered the story nationwide, and southerners did not want northerners to accuse them of judicial malpractice.

As for the insurrection's leader, two black men accidentally discovered Turner in his hiding place and told the whites. Pursued relentlessly, Turner was taken alive at gunpoint. His trial lasted one day and brought swift conviction. From the beginning, Turner probably realized he had little hope for acquittal. With the confidence of a man facing certain death, he described the massacre in bloody detail. His attorney, Thomas R. Gray, was disturbed by Turner's willingness to kill indiscriminately. The murders at Richard Whitehead's plantation were especially shocking. "As I came round the door," Turner told Gray,

> I saw Will pulling Mrs. Whitehead out of the house, and at the step he nearly severed her head from her body with his broad axe. Miss Margaret [Mrs. Whitehead's daughter] . . . had concealed herself in the corner formed by the projection of the cellar cap from the house; on my approach she fled, but was soon overtaken, and after repeated blows with a sword, I killed her by a blow on the head with a fence rail.[31]

Throughout the trial, the man who had caused the death of fifty-seven whites, mostly women and children, displayed no remorse.

The Revolt Inflames White Southerners' Fears

Perhaps this lack of remorse terrified southern whites more than anything. Turner and his men certainly could have escaped. The blacks had discussed entering the Dismal Swamp, a disease-ridden, snake-infested wilderness that sheltered many runaways. From there the slaves could have slipped away to freedom in the North. Not content with freedom, Turner and his men cut a bloody swath across the quiet Virginia countryside killing people they had known for years. One slave killed his master, stripped the socks from the dead man's feet, slipped them onto his own, and proudly paraded about in this grisly attire. Whites might have understood the slaves' actions if they had directed their violence against especially brutal masters, but Turner's men killed any and all whites. At one house, the blacks killed eleven school children while a terrified little girl watched from her hiding place. Turner's revolt was not about freedom. It was about revenge.

Many southern whites who might have had doubts about slavery now felt compelled to take sides. If seventy blacks used their freedom to kill nearly sixty whites indiscriminately, how would three million slaves use their freedom? More than ever, slavery seemed a bulwark against race war. Southern antislavery societies disappeared overnight. The revolt may have destroyed Virginia slaves' best hope for peaceful abolition. Virginia governor John Floyd favored gradual emancipation as a means of modernizing and expanding his state's economy. Even after the Turner revolt, he considered proposing some form of emancipation to the state legislature, but realized that idea had become politically impossible.

Turner's violent revolt struck fear in southerners, ensuring that slaves would not be trusted or granted freedom.

Instead, in December 1831, he recommended more restrictions on blacks. The Turner revolt, he warned, had resulted from a combination of too much black freedom and outside interference. "There is much reason to believe," he said,

> those plans of treason, insurrection, and murder, have been designed, planned and matured by unrestrained fanatics in some of the neighbouring States, who find facilities in distributing their views and plans amongst our population, either through the post office, or by agents sent for that purpose throughout our territory. . . . The most active among ourselves, in stirring up the spirit of revolt have been the negro preachers.[32]

Certainly, Governor Floyd had reason to suspect outside agitation had triggered the revolt. In 1829, a free black in North Carolina had circulated a pamphlet entitled *Walker's Appeal to the Colored Citizens of the World,* which openly encouraged slave revolts. Floyd believed that Turner and other literate black preachers had read and distributed such inflammatory literature. Many white southerners believed this literature included copies of William Lloyd Garrison's *The Liberator* which had began circulating in the South shortly before the rebellion. Convinced that their slaves would not revolt without outside interference, whites began erecting barriers against future slave revolts.

Concerned by the possibility of revolt, a posse of whites shoots at escaping slaves. In an effort to stop slaves from escaping and rebelling, southerners called for increased restrictions on blacks.

Freed slaves are harassed by whites. After the 1831 uprising, many states enacted laws that deterred masters from freeing their slaves.

The Whites Restrict Blacks More Severely

Colonial and state laws had restricted blacks for years, but many of the laws were ignored. In the wake of the Turner revolt, some southern states passed laws making it illegal to teach a slave to read or write or to employ a slave in a print shop. Aware of *Walker's Appeal*, some jurisdictions outlawed the distribution of any literature that might trigger slave insurrection. Judges could now deny jury trials for slaves accused of plotting rebellion, and justices of the peace could impose the death penalty on those convicted. For obvious reasons, slaves could no longer possess firearms.

New state laws also required slaves to possess written passes from their masters giving them permission to leave their plantations. Southern cities imposed strict curfews on slaves. Various laws discouraged masters from freeing their slaves. Remembering that Turner had been a preacher, laws required a white to supervise any slave church service. Some states forbade slaves to gather in large groups for any reason without a white present.

At least in the short term, the Turner revolt moved southern slaves farther away from freedom. The white legal structure struck at the very human rights Americans held most dear: freedom of religion, the right to assemble peacefully, freedom of expression, the right to a jury trial, and the right to arm oneself.

White southerners formed slave patrols to enforce these laws. County courts assigned citizens to serve on these patrols at regular intervals. Patrols searched slave cabins and whipped slaves traveling without permission.

The Turner revolt forced white southerners to deal with some powerful contradictions in their attitudes toward slaves. White southerners commonly argued that slaves were gentle, childlike beings who could not survive outside slavery. Blacks, they argued, happily accepted slavery, and only slavery kept them from returning to their savage African ways. To white southerners it seemed northern abolitionists intentionally endangered their southern cousins.

Blacks also learned from the Turner revolt. Word of the insurrection quickly spread among slaves. No major slave uprising took place in the United States between Turner's revolt and the Civil War. In the twentieth century, historians often refer to Turner's revolt as the United States' only successful slave insurrection. Slaves knew better. They knew the whites had utterly crushed the revolt and killed even those they suspected of involvement. Turner had done worse than fail. He had endangered and brought restrictions on blacks everywhere. The next time a would-be liberator called on the slaves to rise against their masters, few answered the call.

CHAPTER 7

John Brown: Abolitionist Saint

By 1859, slavery had rubbed the nation's nerves raw. Slavery pitted North against South, and neither side trusted the other. Perhaps if a leader who commanded both sections' confidence had emerged, slavery might have ended peacefully, but the leader who emerged at this critical moment was no peacemaker. He preferred conflict to compromise. He was John Brown.

Tensions Rise Between North and South

After the Turner revolt, the slavery debate dominated United States politics. In the 1830s, the possibility of admitting Texas as a slave state triggered debates in Congress that delayed its admission until 1845. The following year, a dispute over Texas's southern boundary sparked war between the United States and Mexico. Victorious in the war, the United States annexed huge tracts of Mexican territory including the future states of New Mexico, Arizona, Colorado, Utah, Nevada, and California. Hoping to halt slavery's expansion westward, in 1846, Congressman David Wilmot proposed legislation banning slavery in the new territories conquered from Mexico. Although it passed in the House of Representatives, the Senate blocked the measure.

As the North's population outgrew the South's it became obvious that only the Senate, where each state had two votes, would reliably stop antislavery legislation. Only by maintaining equality between slave and free states in the Senate could the South deadlock Congress on any issue it chose. California's application for admission as a free state in 1850 threatened the balance. Black slavery had become part of the southern plantation system, a system poorly suited to the arid southwest. For the first time in a generation, the United States had no slave state to balance a new free state in the Senate.

Debate over the issue began when relations between northern and southern members of Congress reached their lowest point.

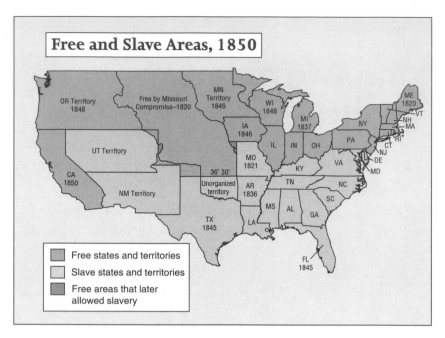

Free and Slave Areas, 1850

OR Territory 1848

Free by Missouri Compromise–1820

MN Territory 1849

WI 1848

ME 1820

VT

MI 1837

NY

NH

MA

UT Territory

IA 1846

IL

IN

OH

PA

CT

RI

NJ

CA 1850

MO 1821

KY

VA

DE

MD

36° 30'

NM Territory

Unorganized territory

AR 1836

TN

NC

MS

AL

GA

SC

TX 1845

LA

FL 1845

Free states and territories

Slave states and territories

Free areas that later allowed slavery

Some southerners openly discussed the possibility of slave states separating from the United States. A number of congressmen and senators, fearing attack by their opponents, carried handguns. Southern congressmen assumed the more densely populated North would eventually control Congress and dominate the South. Once again the forces of unity prevailed. Congress admitted California as a free state and passed a law making it easier for masters to recover slaves who escaped to free states. This Compromise of 1850, as it was called, probably averted a civil war, at least temporarily.

Southerners believed their way of life could only survive if slavery survived and expanded westward. Expansion became possible when Congress passed the Kansas-Nebraska Act permitting settlers to decide whether Kansas would become a free or slave state. Hoping to prevail when the vote finally came, both proslavery and antislavery settlers flooded the territory. Soon armed groups from both sides skirmished with each other. Kansas became so notorious for its violence that easterners called the territory "Bleeding Kansas." It provided the perfect place for John Brown to launch his crusade against slavery.

A Flawed Saint

Before he settled in Kansas, nothing in John Brown's life suggested future greatness. One of sixteen children, Brown was born in Connecticut and grew up in Ohio. His father, a captain in the Revolutionary War, apparently filled him with hatred of slavery. From his earliest years, Brown also professed a devotion to God and his teachings in the Bible. Unlike the Quaker abolitionists, who emphasized God's desire that people repent and turn away from evil, John Brown wanted God to punish sinners.

Although Brown portrayed himself as a righteous man living according to God's will, his life fell short of the mark. He failed in every business he undertook and survived financially by cheating his associates out of thousands of dollars. Not only did Brown spend time in jail for his part in a shady land deal, but he faced twenty-one lawsuits, mostly for financial misdeeds. In his book, *The Impending Crisis: 1848–1861*, historian David M. Potter commented on the contradictions in John Brown's life:

> Throughout the years when these episodes occurred, he constantly expressed the most pious ideals and highminded

Following the passage of the Kansas-Nebraska Act, both opponents and supporters of slavery moved to Kansas, hoping to determine the future of the state.

convictions. . . . [However,] it appears that he did have very high standards but was unable to live up to them. . . . To avoid facing this reality, he began to create an image of himself as a man who was immune to ordinary human frailties; . . . a man of deeds and not words . . . [But] the outward qualities of strength . . . concealed inner . . . weakness—of flawed judgement, homicidal impulse, and simple incompetence.[33]

Despite his flaws, Brown gave his life focus through the antislavery cause. In 1849, he moved his family to North Elba, New York. There he lived in a black community on land donated by wealthy abolitionist Gerrit Smith. Already a father of twenty children, Brown became enthusiastic about adopting a black child and raising him as one of his own.

Brown in Kansas

When in 1855, five of his sons moved to the Kansas Territory, he followed. Brown soon grew impatient with antislavery settlers (also known as "free staters") who wanted to make "Bleeding" Kansas a free state through peaceful means. Brown wanted his pound of flesh. In May 1856, hearing that proslavery forces planned to attack the antislavery town of Lawrence, Kansas, Brown rushed to the settlement's defense with a militia group. Before reaching Lawrence, the antislavery forces learned that proslavery troops had attacked and looted the town. Frustrated in their rescue attempt, most of the free staters went home.

Fiery abolitionist John Brown devoted his life to aggressively fighting slavery.

News of the attack enraged Brown. As the militia dispersed, he assembled four of his sons, one son-in-law, and two other followers into a raiding party. Somehow, the old man mistakenly believed five antislavery settlers had died in the attack on Lawrence. So be it. If five friends of freedom had died, then five proslavery men must die that night—an eye for an eye and a tooth for a tooth. Brown and his men ground keen edges onto their

The savage assault on the abolitionist senator Charles Sumner by proslavery congressman Preston Brooks enraged Brown and strengthened his resolve.

broadswords and set out for the proslavery settlement at Pottawatomie Creek.

On the way, they received word from a rider that a proslavery congressman, Preston Brooks of South Carolina, had taken his cane and beaten abolitionist senator Charles Sumner of Massachusetts on the floor of the Senate. At this news, Brown's men flew into a homicidal fury and hurried on their way. Concealing themselves in the brush along Pottawatomie Creek, Brown and his men made a list of victims and waited for nightfall.

When darkness came the avengers approached an isolated cabin, a dim glimmer of lamplight showing through cracks in the walls. Certain the cabin belonged to a proslaver, Old Brown decided to take revenge here. He hammered on the door with his fist. No one answered, but the raiders could hear the click of a hammer being cocked on a rifle. Fearing the occupants intended to fight, Brown and his men quietly moved on.

Brown and his followers mercilessly murder John Doyle and his sons during their raid on the proslavery settlement of Pottawatomie Creek.

They next approached the cabin of a settler from Tennessee named James Doyle. As before, Brown knocked loudly on the door. This time the door opened and Doyle appeared. Doyle stared into the humorless eyes of a tall, lean man with a full gray beard. It was John Brown, looking like an Old Testament prophet come back to life. Brown ordered Doyle out of the house and marched him away into the darkness.

Two of the raiders stood guard over the settler's wife and three sons. Minutes later, Brown returned and ordered Doyle's sons to come with him. Mrs. Doyle, realizing her husband was surely dead, begged Brown to spare her youngest, a sixteen-year-old. The grim old man agreed and led her older sons from the house. The next day, searchers found the bodies of James Doyle and his two sons nearby. Brown and his men had hacked their victims to death.

After the Doyle murders, Brown led his men to the home of Allen Wilkinson, a member of the territorial legislature. Preparing for bed, Wilkinson stood in his bare feet as he opened the door for Old Brown. One look at Brown's face revealed the old man's murderous mood. Mrs. Wilkinson pleaded in vain for her husband's life, but the raiders dragged him from the house and closed the door behind them. There in the yard, Brown's men cut him down, splitting his skull and stabbing him in the chest. Now Old Brown needed one more victim.

He found his man at the home of James Harris. Harris's house guest, William ("Dutch Bill") Sherman must have fought his attackers as they slashed at him with their broadswords. In the morning, his body lay in Pottawatomie Creek, a stab wound in his chest, his skull opened, and one hand cut off. Brown and his men had washed the blood from their swords in the creek and returned to their homes riding the dead men's horses. That morning as family and friends found the murdered men, Old Brown sat down to his breakfast, clasped his blood-stained hands, and offered a prayer of thanks to God for the food he was about to receive.

Word of the Pottawatomie massacre spread quickly. A proslavery newspaperman named Henry Clay Pate assembled a posse and set out to bring John Brown to justice. Warned in advance of Pate's intentions, twenty-eight free staters rode to Old Brown's defense. Brown put his little army on the road and ambushed Pate's posse. After a battle lasting several hours, the desperate proslavery men surrendered to Brown, later to be rescued by U.S. army troops.

No one ever brought Old Brown to trial for the Pottawatomie murders. On several occasions that summer he crossed the border into Missouri, rescued slaves from captivity, and started them on their way to Canada. In October, he left Kansas to prepare a far bolder strike against slavery.

Eastern Abolitionists Support Brown

From the beginning, wealthy easterners had supplied financial aid, and sometimes weapons, to free staters settling in the Kansas Territory. Now a celebrity among many abolitionists because of his fighting in Kansas, Brown traveled throughout the East asking them for contributions. At first, he told them their money would outfit a small but well-equipped and disciplined force to fight slavery in Kansas. The idea appealed to eastern gentlemen who had done little more than condemn slavery. In Brown, they saw a man of action. Brown carefully cultivated the image, dressing in frontier attire and carrying a large Bowie knife in his boot. He also carried letters of recommendation from well-respected men including former senator and future U.S. Supreme Court chief justice Salmon Chase. During his travels he met with men of national renown including William Lloyd Garrison. Philosophers Ralph Waldo Emerson and Henry David Thoreau hosted Brown in their homes. Old Brown became the toast of New England society.

For all his popularity, he raised barely enough money to meet his own and his followers' needs. Several of his rich benefactors promised large sums they never delivered. Some attempted unsuccessfully to persuade the Massachusetts legislature to provide $100,000 for his activities. He used his limited resources to hire an English military advisor to train his men. He also purchased one thousand pike (spear) heads, weapons useless in mid-nineteenth-century warfare. Untrained troops armed with spears facing disciplined soldiers armed with rifles would have been massacred. The choice of weapons should have warned his followers that Brown did not see the situation realistically.

Brown was rational enough to be disappointed with his meager fundraising. Frustrated, in November 1857, he returned to Kansas to resume his bushwhacking or thuggish ways. On his arrival, he found the antislavery forces in charge of the territory's government. Free staters saw little reason to risk through fighting what they had gained through politics, and they snubbed the leader of the Pottawatomie massacre. Faced with yet another failure, Brown returned to his base in Tabor, Iowa. There he revealed to his followers a plan he had cherished for years.

Brown intended to lead a large-scale raid into Virginia to free slaves. The rebels would then establish a bastion in the Allegheny

A mural entitled The Tragic Prelude *features a larger-than-life John Brown wearing the rugged frontier attire that so impressed eastern abolitionists.*

Mountains where they could repel any attempts to re-enslave them. In February 1858, he discussed the plan with his old friend Frederick Douglass, a man who knew something about slave escapes. Douglass rejected the plan, and Brown rejected Douglass's opinion.

Douglass was right, but Old Brown was persuasive. Six prominent easterners agreed to finance the plot. The "Secret Six," as they came to be known, included New Englanders George L. Stearns, Thomas Wentworth Higginson, Samuel Gridley Howe, Theodore Parker, and Franklin B. Sanborn. The sixth, Gerrit Smith, was the only New Yorker in the group. These men included among their friends poets, senators, and intellectuals. Surely, they realized Brown planned to ignite a revolution.

If the public had paid any attention, they would have anticipated Brown's actions. In the spring of 1858, he held a convention at Chatham, Canada. A small affair attended by about fifty people, most of whom were black, the convention adopted a constitution for a black nation in Virginia's mountains. From their mountain stronghold the blacks planned to incite slave revolts and attack white masters. The convention named Brown commander-in-chief of the army. Old Brown appointed only white officers to lead his future army.

The Attack on Harper's Ferry

Given the convention's small size and its absurd goals, any reasonable observer could dismiss its actions as the work of a lunatic. Sane or not, Old Brown meant to make his dream a reality. In July 1859, he set up housekeeping at a farm in Maryland near the federal arsenal at Harper's Ferry, Virginia. There he assembled his striking force of just over twenty people, a collection of free blacks and several extreme white abolitionists. On the night of October 16, Brown crossed a bridge over the Potomac River from Maryland into Virginia and headed for the arsenal. Appropriately, the self-appointed agent of God's wrath began his march into history on a Sunday.

At first, the liberators met few obstacles. They had to threaten the gatekeeper at the bridge with a pistol before he let them pass. The raiders next approached the railroad depot and found a black man standing watch over the building. When he refused to admit Brown's men, the raiders shot him and entered over his dead body. At least the federal government cooperated. The arsenal, which contained a huge stockpile of arms and ammunition, stood unguarded.

Brown sent detachments to bring hostages including several slave owners into the arsenal. Among them was Colonel Lewis Washington, a relative of the late president. Brown stole a sword

Harper's Ferry, Virginia, where John Brown and his crusaders launched their ill-conceived raid on the federal arsenal.

from the colonel, which Frederick the Great of Prussia had given to George Washington, and strapped it on. One of the hostages, John E. Dangerfield, spoke to Brown and his men. Years after the attack, he described the events at Harper's Ferry:

> I told them [Brown's men] they talked like crazy men. They answered, "Not so crazy as you think, as you will soon see." Up to this time I had not seen any arms; presently . . . the men threw back the short cloaks they wore and displayed Sharps' rifles, pistols, and knives. . . . I saw what, indeed, looked like war—negroes armed with pikes, and sentinels with muskets all around. . . . I asked him [Brown] what his object was; he replied, "To free the negroes of Virginia." He added that he was prepared to do it, and by twelve o'clock [noon] would have fifteen hundred men with him.[34]

For the moment, Brown had only a handful of men, and the citizens of Harper's Ferry, by now aware of the situation, attacked the raiders. Unfortunately, the townspeople had only a few shotguns among them. Several citizens fell to raiders firing from concealed positions. Soon more armed citizens arrived from Maryland, joined the attack, and drove the raiders back into the arsenal.

Brown and his men were trapped. Local militia held the town and the bridges and fired almost continuously on the arsenal for most of the day. Brown seemed unconcerned. While hundreds of bullets thudded into the arsenal's thick walls his men returned fire with their sleek Sharps' rifles. Surrounded by smoke and noise from gunfire, he strolled among the hostages assuring them they would suffer no harm. Brown patiently waited for the black masses to answer his call to freedom. He should have known that very few heard the call. Virginia's slaves did not know that October 16 marked the date for a general uprising. Brown had not told them. The raiders waited for a revolution that would never come.

A Series of Mistakes

Brown was either a bumbler or a madman. In addition to his other mistakes, he had brought no food for his men or his anticipated recruits. Even worse, when authorities later searched his Maryland farm, they found a cache of letters implicating his supporters. Finally, he had placed his men in a town where their enemies had only to seize two bridges to cut off their escape. Brown may have planned to strike a spectacular blow in slave territory and to die a martyr's death. Or Brown may have believed, as many abolitionists believed, that slaves would revolt at the slightest prompting. If so, he couldn't have been more wrong.

Despite all his bungling, the raid could have accomplished more. He could easily have left Harper's Ferry with enough weapons and ammunition to equip a sizeable force before the townspeople knew what had happened. Then he could have traveled from plantation to plantation arming slaves, as Nat Turner had done, and led them to the mountains. Everything depended on speed and surprise. Instead, he dawdled at the arsenal, allowing news of his raid to spread and his opponents to respond.

By nineteenth-century standards the response came quickly. A detachment of U.S. Marines arrived from Washington, D.C., late that night. Their commander, Colonel Robert E. Lee, knowing one rash command could cause the hostages' deaths, delayed. In the morning, he sent twenty-six-year-old Lieutenant J. E. B. Stuart to persuade the raiders to surrender. Old Brown cautiously cracked the door and spoke to the young officer. Having served with the First U.S. Cavalry in Kansas during Brown's bushwhacking days, Stuart recognized Brown immediately. If Brown's presence in Virginia surprised Stuart, his answer to a surrender demand did not. The old man refused.

At a signal from Stuart, the marines charged with fixed bayonets and a battering ram. In an instant, the door fell. Marines poured into the engine house, quickly overwhelming the raiders. Lieutenant Israel Green's light dress sword broke as he cut Old

Brown down. Had Green been better armed, Brown would probably have died at the arsenal that day. Instead he survived to stand trial. Five townspeople, one marine, and twelve of Brown's men died in the fighting. Two of Brown's sons lay among the dead.

Brown on Trial

Both supporters and critics declared Brown mad. Supporters hoped an insanity plea would save him from execution. Critics considered any man who wanted a slave insurrection a lunatic. Brown's relatives provided documents claiming insanity ran in his family, a strategy he disapproved. Long conversations with Brown convinced Virginia governor Henry A. Wise the old man was not only rational enough to face trial but exceptionally brave. Within a week after his capture, Brown faced charges of murder, treason against Virginia, and conspiring to incite slave revolt.

Wounded and lying on a cot, he faced his trial courageously, unlike his fellow conspirators. When his letters appeared in the *New York Herald* and the *New York Times*, some of the "Secret Six" panicked. Gerrit Smith entered an insane asylum to avoid arrest. Howe, Stearns, and Sanborn all took refuge in Canada. Even the normally fearless Frederick Douglass briefly fled the country. Higginson plotted to rescue Brown but abandoned the project when the old man proclaimed his willingness to die.

Marines storm the engine house, forcing Brown and his followers to surrender. Brown was seriously wounded during the skirmish.

Three days before his execution, Old Brown wrote a last letter to his wife and children. As the hour of his death approached, he may have foreseen the consequences of his actions more clearly than any of his contemporaries:

> I am awaiting the hour of my public murder with great composure of mind and cheerfulness; feeling the strong assurance that in no other possible way could I be used to so much advantage to the cause of God and humanity. . . . I have now no doubt but that our seeming disaster will ultimately result in the most glorious success.[35]

For once, Old Brown was right. The Harper's Ferry Raid seemed the greatest of his failures. The attack had alerted slave owners to the possibility of future conspiracies. Brown's followers were dead, captured, or in hiding. But Harper's Ferry helped to divide North and South into warring camps. Thoughtful men such as Ralph Waldo Emerson and Henry David Thoreau publicly praised Brown's raid. Speaking in his defense before Brown's execution, Thoreau said,

> When a government puts forth its strength on the side of injustice, as ours to maintain slavery and kill the liberators

of the slave, it reveals itself a merely brutal force, or worse, a demoniacal force. . . . It was [Brown's] doctrine that a man has a perfect right to interfere by force with the slaveholder, in order to rescue the slave. I agree with him.[36]

Harper's Ferry Divides the Country More Deeply

Such comments convinced many white southerners that prominent northerners, including members of the growing Republican Party, had conspired to ignite race war. An editorial in the *Southern Watchman* warned northerners that incidents such as the Harper's Ferry Raid would bring certain conflict between North and South:

> It teaches a lesson to the fanatics of the North. It shows them that the slaves their misdirected philanthropy would relieve are so well satisfied with their condition that they will not join them in their rebellion . . . [and] that the South can produce hemp enough to hang all the traitors the great "Northern hive" can send among her people to stir up . . . insurrection! . . . It teaches the whole country . . . that the everlasting agitation of the slavery question will inevitably lead to civil war and bloodshed![37]

More moderate northern voices, while still condemning slavery, tried to calm southern fears. Abraham Lincoln rejected Brown's violent tactics and declared his plan so absurd that black slaves refused to share his failure. But southern whites were beyond reassurance. By now they realized that if slavery could not expand into the territories, as Lincoln proposed, the institution and the southern way of life would die. White southerners, like their colonial forefathers, discussed separation from the North and forming militia groups to deal with the northern threat. Brown had made a bloody war to end slavery unavoidable.

When the hangman dropped Old Brown through the scaffold trap door, he executed a murderer and created a martyr. Church bells tolled across the North when Brown died. Nervous southerners, expecting the next northern attack, marched and drilled. Civil war lay just over a year in the future. John Brown had his wish. Six hundred thousand Americans, white and black, would die to purge the land of slavery.

Freedom Born of Violence

Despite horrific loss of life and property, the Civil War freed over three million Americans from bondage. Most abolitionists had hoped the United States would end slavery through peaceful means, but when the fighting began, they embraced the war as a crusade for freedom. Could the abolitionists have adopted a more moderate tone and helped America end slavery peacefully?

Undoubtedly, the abolitionists' harsh attacks on both slavery and slave owners helped trigger the war. By 1860 white southerners considered even the mildest abolitionists supporters of Nat Turner and John Brown. Abolitionist defense of slave revolts and support for Brown helped convince southerners that northerners wanted slaves to slaughter their masters. Not surprisingly, white southerners believed they went to war in self-defense.

Peaceful Alternatives

Ironically, abolitionist agitation prepared slavery's defenders to see Abraham Lincoln as little different from John Brown. Most abolitionists thought Lincoln too timid on the slavery issue. The southern-born Lincoln certainly hated slavery, but intended to block slavery from spreading and in 1862 proposed a plan for gradual emancipation. Under the proposal, the federal government would help the slave states pay masters $400 for each slave freed. All slaves would be encouraged to settle outside the United States. Lincoln's plan left emancipation up to the states and allowed them thirty-eight years to comply.

Congress passed a resolution approving the proposal, and Lincoln presented it to delegates from the border states (the four slave states that remained in the Union: Delaware, Maryland, Missouri, and Kentucky). Most rejected the plan as too expensive. Lincoln assured them that freeing all the slaves in the four states would cost less than three months of war. He also argued that if the Confederate States realized there would be no more slave states to join

President Lincoln and his advisers gather during the signing of the Emancipation Proclamation—the historic document that freed southern slaves.

their cause, they would realize slavery was doomed and give up the war. The delegates remained unconvinced.

The border states' refusal to accept so reasonable a plan disappointed Lincoln. Constant abolitionist pressure may have persuaded Lincoln that he could no longer avoid making the war an antislavery crusade. Certainly Lincoln also hoped England would be less willing to aid or recognize the Confederacy if he called for immediate emancipation. Whatever the motive, his Emancipation Proclamation took effect in January 1863. While it freed only those slaves in areas still rebelling against the United States government, abolitionists realized complete emancipation would surely follow.

Ex-slave Sojourner Truth, a popular figure on the abolitionist lecture circuit, met Lincoln in October 1864. In a letter she dictated days after the meeting, Truth said Lincoln admitted the war had made emancipation possible:

> I said, I appreciate you, for you are the best president who has ever taken the seat. He replied: "I expect you have reference to my having emancipated the slaves in my proclamation. But," said he, mentioning the names of several of his predecessors . . . "they were all just as good, and would have done just as I have done if the time had come. If the

people over the river [pointing across the Potomac] had behaved themselves, I could not have done what I have; but they did not, which gave me the opportunity to do these things." [38]

No Turning Back from Emancipation

Once begun, the war might have forced white southerners to free their slaves even if Lincoln and Congress had not. As the Confederacy exhausted its manpower late in the war, General Robert E. Lee, an opponent of slavery, urged the Confederate government to enlist slaves as soldiers. While units were organized and slaves promised freedom in exchange for their service, none saw action. Nevertheless, the Confederates, whose constitution guaranteed the existence of slavery, had armed men they insisted were property. Armed men would have become citizens. Historians J. G. Randall and David Donald acknowledged the possibility in their book *The Civil War and Reconstruction:*

> There was no mistaking the meaning of this action. The fundamental social concept of slavery was slipping; an opening wedge for emancipation had been inserted. . . . This fact . . . suggests that, even if the Confederacy had survived the war, there was a strong possibility that slavery would be voluntarily abandoned in the South.[39]

Military defeat denied the Confederates that choice. Events moved swiftly following Lee's surrender at Appomattox Courthouse in April 1865. Between December 1865 and July 1868, the United States adopted the thirteenth and fourteenth amendments to the Constitution. These amendments ended slavery throughout the United States and granted blacks citizenship.

The Price of Freedom

The same war that swept away slavery cost both the freedmen and white Americans dearly. Nearly 210,000 blacks served as Union soldiers and sailors during the war. Thousands died in battles such as the assault against Battery Wagner at Charleston, South Carolina, and the Battle of the Crater at Petersburg, Virginia.

If blacks shared white soldiers' suffering, they also shared their poverty. After Appomattox Courthouse, millions of freedmen struggled to make a living in the old Confederate states where most of the fighting had taken place. Four years of war had wiped out nearly half the South's economic capacity. Black families took up their freedom without property, often without education, and without jobs in a devastated land.

A peaceful end to slavery could have avoided this. Most of the countries that permitted slavery accomplished emancipation without war. For example, Britain, a model for American abolitionists, ended slavery through acts of Parliament in gradual stages up to 1833. Cuba outlawed slavery in 1886 and Brazil followed in 1888. Admittedly, gradual, peaceful emancipation delayed freedom, but the resources consumed by the Civil War could have been used more wisely. Freedmen could have received some sort of economic aid with which to start new lives. Southern planters could have been compensated for their loss of slaves and the money used to ease the transition to free labor.

By the mid–nineteenth century southern slaveowners feared even gradual emancipation. White southerners rightly concluded that any kind of abolition meant an end to their way of life. By the 1850s, many white southerners believed free labor yielded greater profits than slave labor and that slavery undermined southern eco-

Homeless and unemployed, blacks congregate in Jacksonville, Florida, years after the Civil War.

nomic development. Even if more white southerners had concluded that slavery hurt the South economically, they would not have embraced abolition enthusiastically. Black slavery guaranteed white social superiority. More important, slavery provided a way of controlling a people that whites simultaneously considered childlike and savage. Living among three million people they both exploited and feared, southern whites were sure to resist violently any attempt to free the slaves.

The Continuing Quest for Equality

A peaceful revolution followed in the Civil War's wake. While many abolitionists such as William Lloyd Garrison initially declared their work done when blacks gained freedom and citizenship, thousands strove to make freedom a practical reality. Frederick Douglass clearly understood that sweeping constitutional amendments alone could not protect the freedmen. The freedmen needed voting rights and education. In *The Life and Times of Frederick Douglass* he wrote:

> The wrongs of my people were not ended. Though they were not slaves they were not yet quite free. No man can be truly free whose liberty is dependent upon the thought, feeling, and action of others; and who has himself no means . . . for guarding . . . and maintaining that liberty. . . . The ballot in the hands of the negro was necessary to open the door of the school house. I used to say, "if the negro knows enough to fight for his country he knows enough to vote; if he knows enough to pay taxes for the support of the government, he knows enough to vote." [40]

Douglass appealed unsuccessfully to President Andrew Johnson to support voting rights for the freedmen. Congress proved more receptive and sent the fifteenth amendment to the states for ratification.

While nationally known leaders such as Douglass championed the freedmen's cause, lesser abolitionists flocked to the South. Many white southerners sneered at them as carpetbaggers (unwelcome northerners who migrated to the South), interfering outsiders. New England schoolteachers educated black children and adults across the old Confederacy. Northern educators recruited black instructors and students for southern schools. Ministers challenged the racial separation in schools, restaurants, and railroad accommodations that prevailed across the South.

Partly due to their efforts (and the presence of the U.S. Army in the old Confederacy), for a generation blacks voted, held office,

Martin Luther King Jr. addresses a crowd of civil rights activists in Atlanta, Georgia. King continued the quest for black freedom that Benjamin Lundy had begun years before.

advanced educationally, and used public accommodations. New state laws passed in the late nineteenth century later undid much of this progress. It would take an ambitious civil rights movement in the 1950s and 1960s to restore black rights.

A Peaceful Revolution

When that time came, America's black population had to make a choice between peaceful and violent agitation. America's most important civil rights leader, Martin Luther King Jr., chose to touch the nation's conscience through a doctrine of love and peaceful action. He and his followers suffered physically at the hands of their persecutors just as Lundy, Garrison, and Douglass had. King faced his modern-day Nat Turners and John Browns. Even at the height of his prestige as a civil rights leader, militant black leaders such as H. Rapp Brown of the Student Non-Violent Coordinating Committee and Huey P. Newton of the Black Panthers urged violent solutions to America's race problem. Early in his career, King had realized armed conflict could only end in a subjugated black minority. In *Why We Can't Wait*, King explained his position:

> During the fifties . . . some called for a colossal blood bath to cleanse the nation's ills. . . . They pointed to an historical tradition reaching back from the American Civil War to Spartacus in Rome. But the Negro in the South, . . . assessing the power of the forces arrayed against him, could not perceive the slightest prospect of victory in this approach. . . . Although his desperation had prepared him with the courage to die for freedom if necessary . . . he was not willing to commit himself to racial suicide. . . . The Negro turned his back on force not only because he knew he could not win his freedom through physical force but also because he believed that through physical force he could lose his soul.[41]

King was right. The 1950s and 1960s saw a flood of court decisions and federal laws advancing black civil rights—court decisions from white judges, laws passed by white legislators, and accepted by a mostly white nation. King and his followers had seared the nation's conscience and won a revolution. Benjamin Lundy would have been proud.

NOTES

Chapter 1: "An Hydra Sin"

1. Stanley Elkins, *Slavery*. Chicago: University of Chicago Press, 1969, pp. 95, 96.

2. Clarence Ver Steeg, *The Formative Years*. New York: Hill and Wang, 1968, p. 192.

3. David Hawke, ed., *U.S. Colonial History Readings and Documents*. New York: Bobbs-Merrill, 1966, p. 334.

4. J. Hector St. John de Crevecoeur, *Letters from an American Farmer*. New York: E. P. Dutton, 1957, pp. 155, 156.

5. Charles M. Wiltse, *The New Nation: 1800–1845*. New York: Hill and Wang, 1968, pp. 9, 10.

6. Mortimer Adler, ed., *The Annals of America*, vol. 5. Chicago: Encyclopaedia Britannica, 1968, p. 510.

Chapter 2: Benjamin Lundy: Pioneer Abolitionist

7. Clement Eaton, *A History of the Old South: The Emergence of a Reluctant Nation*. New York: Macmillan, 1975, p. 371.

8. Merton L. Dillon, *Benjamin Lundy and the Struggle for Negro Freedom*. Urbana: University of Illinois Press, 1966, pp. 102, 103.

9. Dwight Lowell Dumond, *Antislavery: The Crusade for Freedom in America*. Toronto: University of Michigan Press, 1961, pp. 166–67.

10. Henrietta Buckmaster, *Flight to Freedom: The Story of the Underground Railroad*. New York: Dell, 1972, p. 23.

Chapter 3: William Lloyd Garrison: The Uncompromising Abolitionist

11. *The Annals of America*, vol. 5, p. 423.

12. Quoted in George M. Fredrickson, ed., *Great Lives Observed: William Lloyd Garrison*. Englewood Cliffs, NJ: Prentice-Hall, 1968, p. 26.

13. Quoted in Fredrickson, *Great Lives*, p. 43.

14. Quoted in Fredrickson, *Great Lives*, p. 53.

15. Walter M. Merrill, ed., *The Letters of William Lloyd Garrison*, vol. 5: Let the Oppressed People Go Free, 1861–1867. Cam-

bridge, MA: Harvard University Press, 1979, p. 16.

16. Merrill, *The Letters of William Lloyd Garrison*, pp. 271–72.

17. Dumond, *Antislavery*, p. 174.

18. Quoted in Fredrickson, *Great Lives*, p. 89.

Chapter 4: Frederick Douglass: The Voice of His People

19. Frederick Douglass, *The Life and Times of Frederick Douglass*. New York: Citadel Press, 1995, pp. 119–20.

20. Douglass, *Life and Times*, p. 140.

21. Philip S. Foner, *Frederick Douglass*. New York: Citadel Press, 1964, p. 27.

22. *The Annals of America*, vol. 5, pp. 192, 193.

23. *The Annals of America*, vol. 7, p. 422.

Chapter 5: Harriet Tubman: Black Moses

24. Quoted in Sarah Bradford, *Harriet Tubman: The Moses of Her People*. New York: Citadel Press, 1994, p. 24–25.

25. Quoted in Bradford, *Tubman*, p. 24.

26. Quoted in Bradford, *Tubman*, p. 25.

27. Bradford, *Tubman*, pp. 32, 33.

28. Bradford, *Tubman*, pp. 130, 131.

Chapter 6: Nat Turner: Preacher Turned Terrorist

29. *Annals of America*, vol. 5, pp. 474–75.

30. *Annals of America*, vol. 5, p. 474.

31. *Annals of America*, vol. 5, pp. 476–77.

32. Quoted in Henry Irving Tragle, ed., *The Southampton Slave Revolt of 1831: A Compilation of Source Material*. Amherst: University of Massachusetts Press, 1971, p. 432.

Chapter 7: John Brown: Abolitionist Saint

33. Quoted in David M. Potter, *The Impending Crisis, 1848–1861*. New York: Harper & Row, 1976, p. 357.

34. Quoted in Richard Hofstadter and Michael Wallace, eds., *American Violence: A Documentary History*. New York: Vintage Books, 1971, p. 98.

35. Quoted in Richard Warch and Jonathan F. Fanton, eds., *Great Lives Observed: John Brown*. Englewood Cliffs, NJ: Prentice-Hall, p. 100.

36. Quoted in John L. Thomas, ed., *Slavery Attacked: The Abolitionist Crusade.* Englewood Cliffs, NJ: Prentice-Hall, Inc., 1965, pp. 166–67.

37. Warch and Fanton, *John Brown*, pp. 123–24.

Epilogue: Freedom Born of Violence

38. Quoted in Bert James Loewenberg and Ruth Bogin, eds., *Black Women in Nineteenth-Century American Life.* University Park: Pennsylvania State University Press, 1976, p. 237.

39. J. G. Randall and David Donald, *The Civil War and Reconstruction.* Lexington: D. C. Heath, 1969, p. 522.

40. Douglass, *Life and Times*, pp. 385–89.

41. Martin Luther King Jr., *Why We Can't Wait.* New York: New American Library, 1964, pp. 34, 35.

CHRONOLOGY

1619
A Dutch vessel delivers black servants to the Jamestown colony.

1787
The Northwest Ordinance bans slavery in all territory north of the Ohio River and east of the Mississippi River. The U.S. Constitution permits Congress to end slave importation as of 1808.

1789
Benjamin Lundy is born.

1793
Eli Whitney invents the cotton gin.

1800
Nat Turner and John Brown are born.

1805
William Lloyd Garrison is born.

1817
The American Colonization Society is founded.

1819
The Missouri Compromise bans slavery west of Missouri and north of the 36° 30' line.

1820
Harriet Tubman is born.

1821
Benjamin Lundy founds *The Genius of Universal Emancipation*.

1822
The first freedmen settle in the Liberia colony.

1831
William Lloyd Garrison founds *The Liberator*. Nat Turner and his followers murder whites in Virginia.

1833
American Anti-Slavery Society formed.

1837
Abolitionist Elijah Lovejoy killed by proslavery mob in Alton, Illinois.

1845
Texas is admitted as a slave state.

1847
Frederick Douglass founds *The North Star*.

1850
Compromise of 1850 admits California as a free state while enacting a tougher fugitive slave law.

1852
The novel *Uncle Tom's Cabin* is published.

1854
Congress passes the Kansas-Nebraska Act, effectively repealing the Missouri Compromise. The Republican Party is formed.

1855
Fighting over slavery erupts in Kansas.

1856
John Brown murders five proslavery settlers in Kansas.

1857
In the Dred Scott decision, the United States Supreme Court rules that blacks are not citizens.

1859
John Brown raids the arsenal at Harper's Ferry, Virginia.

1860
Abraham Lincoln is elected to the United States presidency.

1861
The Civil War begins.

1863
The Emancipation Proclamation takes effect.

1865
The thirteenth amendment to the United States Constitution ends slavery.

FOR FURTHER READING

Herbert Aptheker, *Nat Turner's Slave Rebellion.* New York: Humanities Press, 1966. Aptheker's account of the rebellion treats Turner as an inspired class revolutionary who hastened the coming of the Civil War.

Sarah Bradford, *Harriet Tubman: The Moses of Her People.* New York: Citadel Press, 1994. Based on conversations with Tubman, Bradford wrote a heroic account of Tubman's exploits on the Underground Railroad.

Henrietta Buckmaster, *Flight to Freedom: The Story of the Underground Railroad.* New York: Dell, 1972. A readable, compact overview of abolitionism, slave escapes, and sectional tensions.

Theophilus Conneau, *A Slaver's Log Book, or 20 Years' Residence in Africa.* Englewood Cliffs, NJ: Prentice-Hall, 1976. This eyewitness account of the slave trade helps the reader understand how people could harden themselves to slavery's horrors.

Richard Conniff, "Frederick Douglass Always Knew He Was Meant to Be Free," *Smithsonian,* February 1995. Conniff's article provides a brief but useful summary of Douglass's life.

Merton L. Dillon, *Benjamin Lundy and the Struggle for Negro Freedom.* Urbana: University of Illinois Press, 1961. In this biography, Dillon has written a detailed and colorful account of the pioneer abolitionist's life. Lundy biographies are comparatively rare.

Frederick Douglass, *The Life and Times of Frederick Douglass.* New York: Citadel Press, 1995. The third version of Douglass's autobiography, this very large, wordy account still inspires modern readers.

Dwight Lowell Dumond, *Antislavery: The Crusade for Freedom in America.* Ann Arbor: University of Michigan Press, 1961. One of the best surveys of abolitionism, this oversize book covers abolitionists often overlooked in other works.

Clement Eaton, *A History of the Old South: The Emergence of a Reluctant Nation.* New York: Macmillan, 1975. A balanced survey of the development of the South's peculiar culture and its ultimate separation from the North.

Stanley Elkins, *Slavery.* Chicago: University of Chicago Press, 1969. Written in the racially charged 1960s, Elkins concludes that blacks in captivity behaved much like white prisoners of war.

Louis Filler, *The Crusade Against Slavery, 1830–1860*. New York: Harper & Brothers, 1960. Filler portrays antislavery as the premier moral crusade of a time when many moral crusades gained momentum in the United States.

Philip S. Foner, *Frederick Douglass*. New York: Citadel Press, 1964. In a complete, insightful, and thoroughly researched biography, Foner declares Douglass one of American history's most important leaders despite his weaknesses.

Daniel Horsmanden, *The New York Conspiracy*. Boston: Beacon Press, 1971. A chilling firsthand account of white fears of slaves and slave resistance to masters in colonial America.

Winthrop D. Jordan, *White Over Black: American Attitudes Toward the Negro, 1550–1812*. Chapel Hill: University of North Carolina Press, 1968. Jordan concludes that whites were reluctant to emancipate black slaves partly because they assumed free blacks would attempt to dominate whites.

Dan Lacy, *The Abolitionists*. New York: McGraw-Hill, 1978. In this concise, readable account, Lacy emphasizes the continuity between the abolitionists and the men and women who sought racial equality in the twentieth century.

Aletha Jane Lindstrom, *Sojourner Truth: Slave, Abolitionist, Fighter for Women's Rights*. New York: Julian Messner, 1981. Intended for younger readers, dialogue and illustrations enliven this biography of an extraordinary woman abolitionist.

Patricia and Fredrick McKissack, *Frederick Douglass: The Black Lion*. Chicago: Childrens Press, 1987. Illustrated with drawings and photographs, the McKissacks have written an energetic biography suitable for younger readers.

Russell B. Nye, *William Lloyd Garrison and the Humanitarian Reformers*. Boston: Little, Brown, 1955. Nye sees Garrison and his abolitionist contemporaries as part of a broader movement to reform and perfect American society in general.

Ann Petry, *Harriet Tubman: Conductor on the Underground Railroad*. New York: Thomas Y. Crowell, 1955. Petry has clarified Tubman's dialect in quotes and fleshed out her story with small details. The result is a small, easily read, and moving biography.

David M. Potter, *The Impending Crisis, 1848–1861*. New York: Harper & Row, 1976. Potter's detailed account explains how America's triumphant march westward helped divide the country and spark the Civil War.

Benjamin Quarles, *Frederick Douglass*. New York: Atheneum, 1968. Aware of the many heroic portrayals of Douglass, Quarles has attempted to define both his strengths and shortcomings.

Kenneth M. Stampp, *The Peculiar Institution: Slavery in the Ante-Bellum South*. New York: Vintage Books, 1956. Scholarly and difficult for young readers, Stampp's book remains one of the most complete accounts of slavery in the old South.

Oswald Garrison Villard, *John Brown, 1800–1859: A Biography Fifty Years After*. Gloucester: Peter Smith, 1965. One of the standard biographies on Brown, Villard's large and scholarly book attempts an unbiased view but proclaims him an inspired martyr.

Margaret Washington, ed., *The Narrative of Sojourner Truth*. New York: Vintage Books, 1993. Actually dictated to Olive Gilbert by Sojourner Truth, this little biography was widely sold on the abolitionist lecture circuit. This volume includes additional documents and appendices.

WORKS CONSULTED

Mortimer Adler, ed., *The Annals of America*. Chicago: Encyclopaedia Britannica, 1968. This multivolume set contains many speeches and articles relating to both sides of the slavery issue.

Arna Botemps, *Free At Last: The Life of Frederick Douglass*. New York: Dodd, Mead, 1971. Like many of Douglass' biographers, Botemps concludes he more realistically gauged the progress of the antislavery movement than most abolitionists.

B. A. Botkin, ed., *A Civil War Treasury of Tales, Legends, and Folklore*. New York: Promontory Press, 1993. A collection of very short, fascinating anecdotes, several of which deal with slaves and freedmen in the Civil War.

Roger Bruns, ed., *Am I Not a Man and a Brother: The Antislavery Crusade of Revolutionary America, 1688–1788*. New York: Chelsea House, 1977. This collection includes antislavery speeches and articles by early abolitionists such as John Woolman and Anthony Benezet, and by patriots such as Thomas Paine.

Bruce Catton, "Black Pawn on a Field of Peril," *American Heritage*, December 1963. In this article, renowned Civil War historian Bruce Catton surveys the Dred Scott case in which the United States Supreme Court declared blacks were not citizens.

Earl Conrad, *Harriet Tubman: Negro Soldier and Abolitionist*. New York: International, 1968. A slender, readable little volume on the life of the Underground Railroad conductor.

J. Hector St. John de Crevecoeur, *Letters from an American Farmer*. New York: E. P. Dutton, 1957. Crevecoeur's reflections on life and labor in the early United States point out the contradictions between Americans' hunger for freedom and their willingness to tolerate slavery.

Frederick Douglass, *My Bondage and My Freedom*. New York: Dover, Inc., 1969. The second of Douglass's autobiographies, this book chronicles events that took place after the publication of Douglass's *Narrative*.

Frederick Douglass, *Narrative of the Life of Frederick Douglass, an American Slave*. New York: Doubleday, 1989. Douglass's first autobiography, it was written largely to convince his critics that he had actually been a slave.

W. E. B. DuBois, *John Brown*. New York: International, 1962. DuBois, one of this century's most famous civil rights advocates, praises John Brown and regrets the old man could not have lived to see Russia and China become communist nations.

George M. Fredrickson, ed., *Great Lives Observed: William Lloyd Garrison.* Englewood Cliffs, NJ: Prentice-Hall, 1968. This book contains documents written by Garrison and his contemporaries.

Larry Gara, *The Liberty Line: The Legend of the Underground Railroad.* Lexington: University of Kentucky Press, 1961. In this thoroughly researched work, Gara provides an accurate and somewhat romantic account of the Underground Railroad.

Hubert Herring, *A History of Latin America from the Beginnings to the Present.* New York: Alfred A. Knopf, 1972. Herring's survey of Latin American history helps provide a broad perspective of slavery and its influence on societies throughout the western hemisphere.

Richard Hofstadter and Michael Wallace, eds., *American Violence: A Documentary History.* New York: Vintage Books, 1971. This collection includes contemporary accounts of slave revolts and an eyewitness account of the Harper's Ferry Raid.

Howard Jones, *Mutiny on the Amistad.* New York: Oxford University Press, 1987. A fascinating account of the most effective sort of slave resistance, sailing a slave ship to freedom.

Alvin M. Josephy Jr., *The Indian Heritage of America.* New York: Bantam Books, 1973. An excellent overview of Native American history, this book also describes slavery before and after whites reached the Americas.

William Loren Katz, ed., *Five Slave Narratives.* New York: Arno Press and the *New York Times*, 1969. This book allows the reader to view slavery from the slave's perspective.

Martin Luther King Jr., *Why We Can't Wait.* New York: New American Library, 1964. Reading King's words helps the modern reader see continuity between the abolitionists and twentieth-century civil rights advocates.

Bert James Loewenberg and Ruth Bogin, eds., *Black Women in Nineteenth-Century American Life.* University Park: Pennsylvania State University Press, 1976. This book includes speeches and writings by women who led in the fight for emancipation and women's rights.

James M. McPherson, *The Abolitionist Legacy from Reconstruction to the NAACP.* Princeton, NJ: Princeton University Press, 1975. McPherson argues that far from abandoning blacks after emancipation, abolitionists led the fight for racial justice in the century following the Civil War.

Jay Monaghan, *Civil War on the Western Border: 1854–1865*. New York: Bonanza Books, 1955. Monaghan describes border conflicts including John Brown's activities in vivid detail.

Truman Nelson, *The Old Man John Brown at Harper's Ferry*. New York: Holt, Reinhart, and Winston, 1973. Nelson's account salvages Brown's raid by arguing that he staged a coup that eventually put antislavery politicians in control of the United States.

Thomas C. Parramore, *Southampton County Virginia*. Charlottesville: University Press of Virginia, 1978. In this regional history, Parramore supplies a detailed account of the Turner revolt while providing background on the area that saw the United States' worst slave uprising.

Lewis Perry and Michael Fellman, eds., *Anti-Slavery Reconsidered: New Perspectives on the Abolitionists*. Baton Rouge: Louisiana State University Press, 1979. The editors intend this collection of essays to provide a balanced image of abolitionists as neither wild radicals nor saintly heroes.

Benjamin Quarles, *Black Abolitionists*. New York: Oxford University Press, 1969. Quarles focuses on black abolitionists that he believes historians have tended to ignore.

Benjamin Quarles, ed., *Blacks on John Brown*. Urbana: University of Illinois Press, 1972. This collection of documents samples the reaction of black Americans to John Brown and his legacy.

J. G. Randall and David Donald, *The Civil War and Reconstruction*. Lexington: D. C. Heath, 1969. One of the best overviews of the subject, Randall and Donald capture the drama of the conflict in a scholarly work.

Edward J. Renehan Jr., *The Secret Six: The True Tale of the Men Who Conspired with John Brown*. While Renehan acknowledges Brown's role in bringing emancipation, he argues that he could have accomplished as much without martyring himself.

John L. Thomas, *Slavery Attacked: The Abolitionist Crusade*. Englewood Cliffs, NJ: Prentice-Hall, 1965. A collection of documents relating to abolitionism.

Henry Irving Tragle, *The Southampton Slave Revolt of 1831: A Compilation of Source Material*. Amherst: University of Massachusetts Press, 1971. Comprised of source documents on the Turner revolt, Tragle's book includes some especially relevant newspaper accounts of the insurrection.

James W. Tuttleton, "The Many Lives of Frederick Douglass," *New Criterion*, February 1994. In this brief biographical article, Tuttleton praises Douglass's willingness to oppose evil. He also wonders whether our society has become too willing to accept wrongdoing.

Clarence L. Ver Steeg, *The Formative Years: 1607–1763*. New York, Hill and Wang, 1968. Ver Steeg's survey of the period supplies background into the origins of the English colonies' social and economic systems.

David Walker, *David Walker's Appeal to the Coloured Citizens of the World*. New York: Hill and Wang, 1995. This booklet's open encouragement of slave violence terrified white southerners in the 1830s.

Richard Warch and Jonahan F. Fanton, eds., *Great Lives Observed: John Brown*. Englewood Cliffs, NJ: Prentice-Hall, 1973. As with all books in this series, this volume contains both documents written by Brown and by contemporaries about Brown.

Charles M. Wiltse, *The New Nation: 1800–1845*. New York: Hill and Wang, 1968. This survey includes useful information about American economic and social developments in the era when cotton became the United States' most valuable export.

John Woolman, *The Journal of John Woolman*, Janet Whitney, ed. Chicago: Henry Regnery, 1950. Woolman's journal gives the reader insights into the antislavery movement's infancy.

INDEX

Picture Credits

About the Author

A native of Elsberry, Missouri, who has taught in public schools for twenty-four years, Stephen R. Lilley holds a master's degree in history. His publishing credits include articles in the *Missouri Historical Review*, *Missouri Life*, and *Highlights for Children*, and two books, *Hernando Cortes* and *The Conquest of Mexico,* published by Lucent Books. He also performs as a traditional jazz musician and has recently released a CD, *Glory Land*. He and his wife, Becky, have two children, Jacob and Sariya, both of whom are published authors.